Public Planet Books

A series edited by Dilip Gaonkar, Jane Kramer,
Benjamin Lee, and Michael Warner

Public Planet Books is a series designed by writers in and outside the academy—writers working on what could be called
narratives of public culture—to explore questions that urgently
concern us all. It is an attempt to open the scholarly discourse
on contemporary public culture, both local and international,
and to illuminate that discourse with the kinds of narrative that
will challenge sophisticated readers, make them think, and especially make them question. It is, most importantly, an ex-
periment in strategies of discourse, combining reportage and
critical reflection on unfolding issues and events—one, we hope,
that will provide a running narrative of our societies at this moment. Public Planet Books is part of the Public Works publication project of the Center for Transcultural Studies, which also
includes the journal *Public Culture* and the Public Worlds book
series.

Sovereignty and Extortion

public planet books

Sovereignty and Extortion

A New State Form in Mexico

Claudio Lomnitz

The 2021 Lectures at El Colegio Nacional

DUKE UNIVERSITY PRESS *Durham and London* 2024

Project Editor: Livia Tenzer
Cover designed by A. Mattson Gallagher
Typeset in Kepler and Eurostile by Copperline Book Services

Library of Congress Cataloging-in-Publication Data
Names: Lomnitz-Adler, Claudio, author.
Title: Sovereignty and extortion : a new state form in Mexico :
the 2021 lectures at El Colegio Nacional / Claudio Lomnitz.
Other titles: 2021 lectures at El Colegio Nacional | Public planet books.
Description: Durham : Duke University Press, 2024. | Series: Public
planet books | Includes bibliographical references and index.
Identifiers: LCCN 2023057418 (print)
LCCN 2023057419 (ebook)
ISBN 9781478030737 (paperback)
ISBN 9781478026495 (hardcover)
ISBN 9781478059721 (ebook)
Subjects: LCSH: Violence—Mexico. | Criminal justice, Administration
of—Mexico. | State, The. | Organized crime—Economic aspects—Mexico. |
Political corruption—Economic aspects—Mexico. | Mexico—Politics
and government—2000– | Mexico—Social conditions—1970–
Classification: LCC HN120.Z9 V5 46165 2024 (print) | LCC HN120.Z9 (ebook) |
DDC 303.60972—dc23/eng/20240410
LC record available at https://lccn.loc.gov/2023057418
LC ebook record available at https://lccn.loc.gov/2023057419

Cover art: Gunther Gerzso, *Presencia* (Presence), 1962. Oil on Masonite,
65.4 × 50.5 cm. Photo © Christie's Images/Bridgeman Images. Original
© John Michael Gerzso 2013.

Contents

Preamble

This book brings together the six lectures that I delivered in my first year as a member of Mexico's El Colegio Nacional (2021). My aim in these lectures was to use ideas and concepts from social anthropology to offer a structural interpretation of the extreme violence that Mexico is currently suffering. The book's thesis is that a new type of state has been developing in Mexico. It began to take shape during the neoliberal reforms of the 1980s and 1990s, then consolidated with the start of the war on drugs launched by the government of Felipe Calderón in 2006, and has continued to develop in the current, post-neoliberal moment. The true nature of this new state contrasts with both of the two master narratives that dominate Mexican public discussion: the story of the "democratic transition," on the one hand, and Andrés Manuel López Obrador's tale of a so-called Fourth Transformation, which paints the current popular-authoritarian turn as the culmination of Mexico's centuries-long struggle for sovereignty, on the other. Each of these historical frameworks presumes the existence of a state that is altogether different from the one that actually exists. Specifically, they share the precept that the Mexican state is capable of administrating justice—and, in particular, criminal justice—within a legal framework. They also subscribe to the notion that the Mexican state is capable of regaining the monopoly of the legitimate use of force. Finally, both narratives assume that the violence that plagues the country is merely an interlude—it is a "war on drugs," for instance, or a side effect of the inequality induced by neoliberal reform—that will conclude with the reestablishment of a peace that shall be similar to the one that once existed.

My starting point, on the contrary, is that what is happening in Mexico is not a confrontation that can end with a winner and a loser. It is not a war against crime that the state can either win or lose. Rather, we are facing a new way of governing. A new way of life.

The analysis that develops throughout the chapters of this book oscillates between a focus on this new state and a probe of the social breakdown that is characteristic of the era. This social breakdown is frequently attributed to a moral crisis, to the unravelling of community and of family mutuality. This is the so-called torn social fabric. In order to understand the conditions of both moral revolt and dissolution, I have tried to define the relevant changes in economics, authority, and public safety that are the foundation of our contemporary mores, and of the values that go with them.

Because this book brings into print a cycle of public lectures, its style diverges from the density that is typical of texts written for a readership of specialists. I wrote these texts with the aim of enriching public discussion, albeit always from an anthropological vantage point. Given this objective, I kept allusions to the academic debates that are relevant to each of the topics to a minimum, retaining only the references that I found indispensable to build a line of argumentation.

During the eleven months of work that is condensed in these chapters, I was privileged to consult with colleagues who know much more than I about many of the subjects that I cover. I am especially grateful to Elena Azaola, Naor Ben-Yehoyada, José Ramón Cossío, Fernando Escalante, Alejandro Madrazo, Salvador Maldonado, and Fernando Montero. This book also benefited from discussions in the Violence and New Mores Workshop that I led at Columbia University's Center for Mexican Studies in 2020–21, as well as from the presentation of Alejandra Azuero at the Evasion Workshop co-organized by the Universities of Toronto, Michigan, Columbia, and Princeton, whose ideas about *hedging* as a modality of evasion provided a clue that led to one of the ideas presented in my sixth lecture.

Finally, I would like to acknowledge the generosity of El Colegio Nacional, which has provided me with the platform and audience required to pursue my long-held commitment to deploy the instruments of my discipline to further our understanding of the pressing issues of our public life.

1 Interpretation of the "Torn Social Fabric"

The Question of the "Social Fabric"

t is common to attribute Mexico's violence to a "tear in the social fabric." At an intuitive level, the image seems adequate, since today's violent outbreaks crush our most entrenched values: kidnappings trample our ideals of liberty; rape violates personal integrity; murder extinguishes the right to exist; and the deliberate dismemberment of corpses mangles the dignity of those who are defenseless. Finally, the forced disappearance of a person—and today (November 2021) there are officially more than 93,000 disappeared in Mexico, a number that increases daily—forecloses even the customary and universally espoused right to mourn a loved one. All of these transgressions are routinely suffered in contemporary Mexico, and we lack even a widely shared narrative or epic that is capable of recognizing, processing, and beginning the work of putting an end to these outrages.

Sometimes we characterize what is happening as a "war on drugs," but it is not exactly that. The Trojan War had an end:

the capture of Helen and the sacking of Troy, and the victory of the Achaeans. The so-called war on drugs, on the other hand, has no real finality, because drugs are powerful substances that, like the famous *pharmakon* of the ancients, are at once a poison, a remedy, and a scapegoat. It is impossible to defeat a thing that is both a poison and a cure, much less to vanquish an enemy who serves the useful role of the scapegoat. The addict sees heroin as a cure for her pain, though she knows that her addiction will lead to her own death. To take away the addict's drug is to rob the helpless. For his part, the peasant who grows opium poppies amid his cornfields also knows of the danger that this crop brings with it, but he understands, too, that it is only thanks to *it* that he and his family can scrape through the year. Like heroin for the addict, the farmer's poppies, too, are both a problem and a solution, a poison and a cure. And since our "good society" seems convinced that criminality emanates from drugs and the drug trade, the imprisonment or killing of producers, addicts, and distributors becomes an expiatory act for a society that doesn't know how to secure its own collective well-being. The so-called war on drugs allows Mexican society to set aside the many causes of its many ills.

Given the multiple uses of both drugs and the various actors who are involved in the drug economy, there can be no real war, because there can be neither victor nor vanquished. Mexico is thus entangled in a conflagration that has a ritual purpose, a new edition of the Aztecs' "Flowery War," perhaps, whose captives are served up as sacrificial victims. More than a war, Mexico's current violence is a way of life, and it has as its counterpart a new state that still doesn't know what to call itself or how to tell the story of its own origin. We are witnessing the Flowery War of a people that has not yet invented its tutelary god, of an empire that has not yet named its true champion, that has not yet invented its Huitzilopochtli.

I say that it is a state that does not know what to call itself because when, in 2006, the government of President Felipe Calderón launched its war on drugs, it did not ask (and no government has asked since) whether the Mexican state, that still fancies itself a democracy, had or has the financial resources required to eradicate the drug economy with measures and means that are consistent with the law. Did Mexico have the police, detectives, forensic experts, judges, and well-conditioned prisons that would have been required to capture and legally process the delinquents who were involved in the drug economy? As I said, this question has not been raised in the fifteen years since the start of the drug war. Had it been raised, the answer would have been a resounding "No." As a result, the state that is waging this war on drugs is necessarily governed by something other than the rule of law. And neither did the government have the resources to build up alternative economies for the peasants, ranchers, low-level drug dealers, scouts, couriers, and hit men who work in the drug economy. Nevertheless, the government loosed a military offensive against an economy that, as we have already remarked, produces a commodity that is both a poison and a cure.

That decision generated a brutal increase in violence, not only because there were now many more armed confrontations between delinquents and soldiers, but also because Mexico's armed forces overrode the work of mediation that had until then been carried out by the ancien régime's poorly funded but always present police and judges and prosecutors. As the old mechanisms for regulating illicit acts fell by the wayside, morality itself became a tactical objective. The everyday customs of various communities, together with the ideas about right and wrong to which they were attached, attracted the strategic attention of armed groups that could only build brief truces and a brittle peace in their constant strife for territorial control.

The outrages that are routinely perpetrated against familial and communitarian mores have been such that they have left us speechless, and so we blame the morality that is meant to uphold those customs: we say that it has been corrupted, that the social fabric has been torn, and we try to find the hidden springs of our new violence in that tear. Stunned by the daily atrocities that resonate in the public sphere, we reach back to the old pillars of communitarian morality as a final recourse. We have seen some plead to the mothers of the drug lords, so that they might do their bit to stop their sons' violence, appealing to the most primordial of all communitarian bonds—the relationship between mother and son—with the hope that this most sacred talisman might be capable of recovering human decency and of staging a collective return to sanity.[1] When that strategy failed, we then heard the president of the republic preach from his podium—that pinnacle of patriarchal authority—calling on Mexico's wayward youth to straighten themselves out and reminding them that perhaps they had forgotten their parents' most elemental lessons. He tried to rescue the distinction between right and wrong with the sort of admonition that Mexican parents use when they speak to their children: "Violence is *fuchi*"(stinks or is disgusting), "violence, *guácala*" (makes you want to gag or throw up). These reprimands were spoken by President Andrés Manuel López Obrador after his landslide electoral victory of 2018, when he still believed that he could resolve all matters pertaining to security in a matter of months.

Like Mexico's president, those who make appeals to morality imagine that the people who perpetrate violent acts have not been properly socialized, or perhaps they have forgotten their parents' teachings and so, maybe now, might hear the chiding that comes from the lips of someone who is looking out for them and is willing to take the place of the absent father: the president of the republic. These invocations appeal to that which is most sacred—they are done in the name of the mother or in the name of the father—and they thereby sound a desperate call to preserve the very foundation of society: the family. And when that fails—as it has already failed—we then claim that there is a tear in the social fabric.

In their book on cloth as artifact and symbol, anthropologists Jane Schneider and Annette Weiner argued that, as a frequently used metaphor for the idea of community, cloth highlights the strength that is found in interdependence, but the metaphor also suggests a kind of fragility of the individual.[2] The image of fabric invokes mutual aid and reciprocity as the foundational principles of the social, while it also recognizes that, like threads, social connections can easily be cut.

Today in Mexico it is common to say that there is a tear in the social fabric. This claim is grounded in the idea that the most intimate forms of interdependence have broken down; family values are regularly ignored, communities are weak. This does not necessarily imply that social relations have been strained because of social inequality. Indeed, according to Max Weber, communitarian relations do not imply equality but rather the recognition or feeling of being a part of the same thing. This is why members of communities often rely on organic metaphors to describe the nature of their interconnections: the community is like a body, for instance, or like an organism, and its parts are as different from one another as the head is different from the heart or the arm. And it is precisely for this reason—because the idea of community relies on complementarity rather than equality—that communitarian relations develop numerous mechanisms for mediation, compensation, and exchange. The image of community as a social fabric exalts both the strength and the fragility of these mechanisms of mediation, but when—as today—we don't understand why communities have become so enfeebled, we make appeals not so much to those mechanisms of mediation and compensation as to the bonds that are thought to be most sacred: we appeal to the mothers or to the sacred tenets of the Church, or we rely on the persuasive force of the Great Patriarch, the president of the republic. Except that none of this seems to be working.

Sovereignty versus State

In a recent book on the anthropology of kings and kingship, David Graeber and Marshall Sahlins suggest the utility of separating the study of sovereignty from the many other attributes that are frequently attached to the idea of the state, such as the monopoly of the legitimate use of force or the administration of justice.[3] Through their rich comparative studies of the figure of the king, Graeber and Sahlins show that sovereignty has existed in societies that lacked public administration, where there was no monopoly of the legitimate use of force, and where various other attributes that are usually considered essential features of the state are weak or absent. Indeed, these two anthropologists show that sovereignty historically precedes the development of the state.

Our authors argue that, from a cultural point of view, there never was such a thing as an egalitarian society, because even those societies without internal stratification inhabit social worlds in which humans coexist with spirits or gods who are, in the words of Graeber and Sahlins, "metapersons" who wield sovereign power over the lives and deaths of the members of the community. In other words, the societies that we sometimes call egalitarian existed in a universe that they recognized as hierarchical.

Put another way, small-scale human societies seem always to have imagined themselves as existing in a world that has been populated by multiple sovereigns, and even when society itself lacked such figures, the fate of the people relied on negotiations with metapersons—gods and spirits—who needed to be avoided, appeased, or coaxed, and who might always intervene on their own volition. Often this sort of worldview developed together with a corresponding metaphysical topography, with beings moving between two or more planes or spheres—for instance, between one that is terrestrial, another that is subterranean, and a third that is celestial. The figure of the terrestrial king is always fashioned in imitation of metapersons who originate in other spaces, and the intervention of such metapersons has always preceded the birth of the king and the creation of a kingly line. Graeber and Sahlins thus turn the classical sociological idea that the divine world imitated the human world on its head: historically, kings have imitated gods, and not the other way around.[4]

As a corollary, our authors conclude that among humans authority is never truly secular: as an idea, sovereignty always has a foreign, outworldly origin. Because of this, although kings are gods of sorts, the gods always transcend the personality of any one king. A second corollary, which is important to us here, is that sovereignty does not need perforce to go hand in hand with that bundle of attributes that is usually associated with the state. There are gods where there is no state, and there have been kings who have presided over truly squalid administrative structures, with neither a police force nor an army at their disposal.

These ideas, which appear to be so distant from the concerns of contemporary Mexicans, in fact offer us a useful entry point because over the past couple of decades the Mexican state has shed some of its "classical" attributes. And for this reason, we sometimes imagine the violence that has emerged as a symptom of a "failed state," when in fact we might think of it as an attribute of a new kind of state. Furthermore, the mistaken idea that we are just a small step away from state failure has gone hand in hand with an obsession to "recover" Mexico's sovereignty— an obsession that is expressed in the current government's outlandish, even ruinous, subsidies for the national oil company (Petróleos Mexicanos; PEMEX) and the national electric company (Comisión Federal de Electricidad; CFE), and especially in its extravagant support for the army, whose budget quadrupled between 2013 and 2018, and has grown much more steeply since then; for the navy, whose budget more than doubled in those same years and has also continued to climb; and for the National Guard that was created in 2018 and now has around triple the number of officers as the Federal Police, which it was created to substitute.[5] The current obsession with the "recovery of our sovereignty" is in fact unnecessary because one of the few attributes that the Mexican state has *not* shed is its demonstrated ability to perform sovereign acts. Thus, even though the Mexican state has utterly failed its duty to administer justice in criminal matters, its presidents still speak in the name of the nation without being challenged anywhere; and they cede more and more responsibilities to the nation's armed forces, even while the military has shown itself to be incapable of effectively regulating violence at the local level. Indeed, today's state is marked by an *excess of sovereignty and a deficit of administrative capacity.* This, in a nutshell, is the nature of Mexico's new state.

The country's armed forces often experience and suffer from this combination of heightened sovereignty and diminished administrative capacity. Journalists Daniela Rea and Pablo Ferri have documented the extrajudicial killings by the military in its war on drugs, and Rea and Ferri's work offers many examples of such experiences. One of the soldiers that they interviewed explained the practice of extrajudicial killings as follows: "Even if you take them [captured drug lords or gang leaders] to the judge with confessions, and with their hands and bodies covered in blood, they let them go. We did this [killed them] because of the people who they had killed."[6] A bit further into this same interview, the soldier completed his explanation of the nature of his actions: "What I did was justice. Vengeance is personal. This was justice."[7]

For this soldier, then, there is no justice if it is not extrajudicial, executed directly by the army, which is the representative par excellence of national sovereignty. Execution at the hands of the armed forces is therefore not personal vengeance or any other kind of abuse of power but rather an act of justice, done in the name of the people of Mexico. Extrajudicial executions are then a symptom of the surfeit of sovereignty, not of its lack: the army is capable of taking justice into its own hands without any real contest precisely *because* the state lacks credible institutional ability to administer justice. If the military were to hand the criminals whom they catch over to the law, they would be let go. Justice must then be administered extrajudicially, by the sovereign's armies.

Explanations of the military's routine use of torture follow this same logic. Rea and Ferri summarize the views of another one of their interviewees: "He knows that it is morally and legally wrong to torture but believes that in Mexico the use of torture is a corrective measure that is practiced in lieu of legally administered punishment, which is always either improbable or too slow in coming."[8] This soldier's perspective—which is far from unusual—reveals some of the reasons for the inordinately high lethality rates that have been typical in confrontations between Mexico's armed forces and organized crime and that have been denounced by social scientists who have tracked these statistics.[9]

Violence and Reciprocity

Although gratuitous acts of violence do exist, violent acts are rarely lacking in either a past or a future that can be used to justify them. To kill without provocation and without suffering any negative consequences is a sovereign act. And when impunity is routinized and carried out by a collectivity, the violence that is exercised by those who suffer no consequences gives way to the formation of castes.

So, to recall one historical instance of this, Christopher Columbus described the inhabitants of the islands that he discovered in the following terms: "They have no weapons, and they go about naked, and have no ingenuity with regard to arms, and are very cowardly, so that one-thousand of them would not stand up to three [of ours], and so they are well suited to be commanded and made to work, to plant, and to do whatever else might be needed, and to build towns, and be taught to go about clothed and to adopt our customs."[10]

The invincibility of European arms in America gave way to a frenzy of violence that had few limits, other than those imposed from within the dominant camp itself. And where there is such impunity, there is also sovereignty, and that led to the confirmation of an idea of group superiority. There is an element of such caste superiority present also in the so-called narco culture, where the drug lords (*señores*) strive to give shape to a new caste that has prerogatives and attributes distinct from those of the people who are in their service. We will return to this matter later.

For now, it is worth underscoring that impunity on this scale is infrequent, and that in the majority of cases violence gets inscribed in a logic of reciprocity or, to be more precise, in a type of reciprocal relationship that anthropologists have called "negative reciprocity." The paradigmatic form of this sort of reciprocity is the feud, where assassination leads the kin of the victim to seek blood compensation. When there is no state that is capable of performing this duty, the brethren of the victim take the matter into their own hands and kill either the murderer or one of his kinsmen. This counter-assassination then provokes a new round of aggressions, and the two groups embrace in a spiral of violence. According to René Girard, the ancient institution of sacrifice was a remedy precisely against this sort of spiraling violence; the scapegoat distracted aggressions away from the heart of society and toward a weaker third party, thereby avoiding the ungoverned contagion of reciprocal aggressions.

Normatively, state action is supposed to be geared against the two extremes that we have discussed—total impunity and reciprocal violence—and thus is supposed to reduce the autonomy of violent actors, gain a monopoly over the administration of justice, and so guarantee that societal violence will neither go unpunished nor be claimed directly by those closest to its victims. In Mexico, however, the state was unable to consolidate such a position and the institution known as *caciquismo*, in which the state deposits the local administration of justice and regulation of violence in the hands of an intermediary who is not a bureaucrat, is a symptom of this historical fact.

In consideration of this administrative arrangement, a few years ago I proposed a second modality of negative reciprocity that is distinct from the symmetry that characterizes feuds, which I called "asymmetrical negative reciprocity." This term describes a form of exchange that is initiated with an act of violence—a rape, a beating, or a murder, for instance—that is performed against a person or group that does not have the capacity to respond in a proportional manner, and that also has no recourse to the state for protection.[11] Such violent acts are then followed immediately by a small or symbolic gift, or perhaps by some personal consideration or concession, that gives way to a longer-term relationship of submission. Asymmetrical negative reciprocity is used, then, to establish relationships of domination that originate in acts of violence but are then routinized as relationships framed by debt (represented by the small gift or concession that follows the violent act). This sort of violence generally does not lead to the formation of a new caste, because it is limited in its sphere of action both by a (weak, but still present) state and by local competition, but it does serve to build local hierarchies. It is the world of novelist Juan Rulfo's *Pedro Páramo*, where the entire village is symbolically related (kin) because all villagers are victims of the violence of the same cacique. In Juan Rulfo's fictional village of Comala, everyone is a child of the cacique Pedro Páramo. But the power of the cacique is not the point of origin for a new caste as much as the hinge between a weak state and a rural community.

If we keep in mind these three ways of exercising violence— the sovereign form, symmetrical negative reciprocity of the sort expressed in feuds, and asymmetrical reciprocity of the kind that develops in caciquismo—we can make some headway into specifying the developments that are today figured in a general and imprecise way under the simile of a "torn social fabric."

Toward a Geography of Negative Reciprocity

Today's violence in Mexico can be better understood if we analyze it in reference to the different kinds of negative reciprocity that are used to articulate a complex economic geography. I illustrate this notion with a couple of cases so that the idea becomes clearer.

My first example concerns a discussion that transpired in the 1990s scholarly literature regarding the question of whether the heroes of the so-called *narco-corridos* (narco-ballads) conformed to the prototype of what historian Eric Hobsbawm had famously called "social bandits," that is, popular figures who stole from the rich and gave to the poor. Certainly, the image of drug lords as benefactors has some resonance, but the complex geography of the illicit economies that they articulate in fact precludes any stable characterization of their connection to either "the people" or "the poor."

Take, for instance, the well-known case of Rafael Caro Quintero, a prominent drug lord who was the protagonist of many narco-ballads and had a reputation as a benefactor in his home community of La Noria, as well as in the municipal seat of Badiraguato, Sinaloa, where he paid for roads, funded schools, and introduced various urban services. From this vantage point, then, Caro Quintero fits the type of the social bandit, but Caro was also the owner of a 544-hectare plantation known as El Búfalo, in the nearby state of Chihuahua, where he planted marijuana with the connivance of both the Federal Police and the Mexican army. That ranch was eventually discovered by agent Kiki Camarena of the US Drug Enforcement Administration

(DEA) and his associate, the Cessna pilot Alfredo Zavala, and as a result they were both kidnapped, tortured, and murdered. In response, the DEA pressured the Mexican army to take possession of El Búfalo ranch and, when that happened, the public learned that it was run with the labor of several hundred peasant captives. They had been lured there from distant states under false pretenses and now lived on the premises and were forced to work under the watch of armed guards, who did not allow them to leave the ranch. In this example, then, Caro Quintero engaged in patron-client ties on his home turf, where he operated as something like a social bandit, while he was a slaveowner in a more distant territory.

A second example can help expand our field of inquiry into the connection between the complex geography of illicit economies and forms of communitarian or anticommunitarian violence.

Studies of the gangs known as *maras* in Los Angeles, California, have described them—and particularly their component cliques, known in Spanglish as *clicas*—as quasi-families. They operate with an ideology one early ethnographer dubbed "democratic anarchy," where there are no fixed leaders or any internal chain of command.[12] Rather, violence is organized around *jales* (jobs, adventures) that are adhered to more or less spontaneously and in voluntary fashion.

The quasi-familial nature of these gangs in the 1990s made it imperative for members to go out in defense of any other member and also to defend the gang's home neighborhood. Indeed, the relationship between gang and neighborhood was very important, and gangs generally tried to stop their own members from stealing from or raping people from the neighborhood. In short, these gangs drew sharp distinctions between an inside and an outside, and that was relevant for both gang and neighborhood identity.

Gang members say that they lead *la vida loca* (the crazy life), which is a lifestyle that involves a kind of "deep hanging out," wherein leisure is punctuated by occasional *jales* (often joint ventures involving illegal activity), violent episodes, and public displays of valor. However, gang members can also do work for other, more disciplined and hierarchical organizations, like that of Caro Quintero in his time. For this reason, there are gangs and gang members who end up obeying instructions from bosses in relationships that are neither democratic nor anarchic in nature. Up until the point when a gang gets tied financially to a cartel, it operates as an informal organization that offers *clica* members a sense of belonging and free access to *la vida loca*, as well as protection for their neighborhood or ethnic group (recall that *Salvatrucha* is actually an injunction, that translates into something like "Heads up, Salvadoran!"). Once a neighborhood gang relies on a cartel, however, it becomes an instrument of control over the barrio that is exercised, in the last instance, by actors who have no special connection to the neighborhood.

Here again we see two contrasting ideologies of reciprocity coexisting: the reciprocal ties of brotherhood within the gang, and the transactional business ethos fostered by criminal business organizations of the sorts that are known today as cartels. As a result, a *mara* can be at once the defender and the aggressor of the "social fabric" of its own neighborhood. These are instances of the sort of ambiguities that we must describe in order to develop a geography of violence, and through it to understand the complex connections that exist between various kinds of violent actors and the social fabric.

The third example of complex geographies of violence that I wish to consider concerns stealing women, and it requires more careful elaboration.

Historical Arc of Stealing Women in Mexico

We do not yet have a proper history of the practice of stealing women in Mexico. My considerations here are limited to a 17 few examples from the twentieth century that reveal a "traditional" set of practices, which I shall then use to contrast with two more contemporary modalities. In order to understand what is at stake, though, we need to linger for a moment on the marriage practices that served as the framework that originally gave meaning and purpose to bride theft.

One common formula for normatively sanctioned marriages in rural nineteenth- and twentieth-century Mexico had the following characteristics: first off, weddings were expensive, and they required resources from both the parents of the bride and the parents of the groom. After the marriage, the newlyweds preferentially established residence in the same plot as the groom's parents (virilocal residence) and hoped one day to inherit from them a plot where they might build their own house. These customs meant that brides usually entered matrimonial life as subordinates of their mothers-in-law, and there was much competition between daughter-in-law and mother-in-law for the groom's favor, a trend that has long been a factor in the formation of male and female subjectivities in rural Mexico.

In addition, because weddings were relatively expensive, young couples began their married lives indebted either to the parents of the groom or to those of the bride or to both, or, sometimes, to a patron who paid the cost of the wedding. For instance, in late-nineteenth-century Yucatán, hemp-growing landowners typically paid for their workers' traditional Maya wedding ceremonies. Freighted with that debt, the young married couples then settled on the land of the plantation owner as indentured laborers. In such cases, the landowner took the place of the father of the groom, and the plantation became the place to which the young couple would devote its life's work.

One can easily understand the attraction of bride theft in the face of practices such as these. By obviating the expensive marriage ritual, young couples who eloped could live together without the yoke of a major debt toward parents or surrogate parents. Stealing the bride was also a viable path to marriage in situations where the families of the bride and groom did not see eye-to-eye with each other. The victim of this sort of bride theft (*robo de la novia*) was thus not the young woman or girl who was being "stolen"—she was a party to the stratagem—but rather her parents, who would lose a daughter without gaining the recognition and prestige that went along with an elaborate communal marriage ceremony.

Since the aggrieved party was the parents of the bride (and not the bride herself), the parents of the groom frequently took it upon themselves to visit the parents of the bride after their daughter's theft and beg them to forgive their children and to accept them as man and wife. Sometimes the groom's parents brought a mediator along, who was usually a kinsman of both of the families, or, as in a case described in depth by anthropologist Paul Friedrich in the Tarascan region of Michoacán during the late 1950s, the mediator might be a cacique, who was recognized by all as a force in the local order, and who often was also well versed in elaborate local formulas of courtesy and tact.[13] In those same years, anthropologist Hugo Nutini described marriage practices in a Nahuatl-speaking village in Tlaxcala where bride theft was frequently practiced. There, both the parents of the groom and the parents of the bride were expected to make a show of anger when a bride was "stolen," since anything short of such formal expressions of displeasure might suggest to the wider community that perhaps the parents did not have the money to pay for the wedding, and that they secretly approved the young couple's transgression of the local norm.[14]

So far, then, the practice of bride theft appears as a relatively benign custom that reduced the yoke of marital debt and facilitated the free choice of a marriage partner. Nonetheless, the custom known as *robo de la novia* also had other, more violent, modalities that, in legal terms, might easily have been prosecuted as kidnappings and rapes.

This second kind of bride theft began with a young man eyeing a young woman who was not interested in him. The young man would then organize a kidnapping party, forcefully abduct the woman (often at gunpoint), take her to the house of one of his kinsmen, and rape her. After that, just as in the cases of consensual "bride theft," the feat was made public, so that the entire community knew about the theft, making it an established fact.

In cases of this nature, the presence of a mediator was often indispensable to calm the animus of the parents of the "bride," and to reduce the likelihood of violence breaking out between the families. Because of the signal importance of mediators in such cases, the parents of the "groom" (rapist) often had to pay the mediator money. Both in the Tarascan case described by Friedrich and among the Nahua peasants described by Nutini, the parents of these unfortunate young women tended in the end to be appeased and to recognize the young couple as husband and wife.

In short, regardless of the bride's consent, the final outcome of bride theft was similar: the young couple would be married. It is worth noting that the same general formula—bride theft—was used to refer to both of these practices, despite the fact that in one case the bride was party to the decision, whereas in the other she was coerced.

The reason why two such contrasting situations were lumped together into a single formula (*robo de la novia*) was that, as noted, the victims of the theft were thought to be the parents of the young woman and not the woman herself. It was for this reason that the parents needed to be appeased much more urgently than the "bride"; presumably she would later be made to comply by her new husband. The community as a whole was mobilized in order to assuage the feelings of the parents of the bride, since the groom's parents' persuasive ability leaned on the informal connections that existed between the two families—either through indirect family ties or due to pressure from the local political boss or cacique. In other words, the "social fabric" was used to bring the parents of the girl, and eventually the girl herself, into line.

In sum, the solution to the social conflicts that bride theft let loose hinged on the dependence that daughters and sons had on their parents, and on the relationship between the two families as they might be mediated by their shared village membership. The social fabric that we are sometimes so very nostalgic about today has not always been as kind as we imagine, and it has frequently exhibited a penchant to sacrifice the weak at the altar of communal harmony.

Stealing Women Today

In contrast to the two "traditional" practices of *robo de la novia* that we have described thus far, today the degree of dependence of rural youth with regard to their parents is much reduced, thanks to which a girl and a boy who wish to marry or live together can usually do so without their parents' permission and with little need for mediation. If the young couple is not accepted, it can also emigrate, often with relative ease. This is due not only to the opening up of the labor market for women—a market that had been quite restricted until the early 1980s—but also to the fact that today farming tends to provide only an income supplement, rather than a full family income.[15]

On the other hand, if a man kidnaps a young woman and rapes her with the intention of living with her, it remains to be seen whether community relations would be strong enough to enforce the union. Today, if an abducted woman manages to escape from her assailant, she can accede to a salary much more easily than in the contexts described by Friedrich or Nutini for the mid-twentieth century. On the other hand, if a young couple seeks to live together without their parents' consent, the role of rural inheritance has declined sufficiently to make this step relatively tempting. Finally, the consolidation of the Mexican state and the rise of women's rights have made it easier for a woman or for her parents to initiate prosecutions, so that the young rapist might find himself having to flee his village or face possible imprisonment.

In principle, then, the decline of peasant economies, the urbanization of the countryside, and the integration of women into labor markets should all be factors leading to the disappearance of the practice of bride theft in either of its two modalities. Nevertheless, as anthropologist Adele Blázquez has recently demonstrated in her extraordinary ethnography of daily life among opium poppy growers in the municipality of Badiraguato, Sinaloa, there are regions in today's Mexico where a significant proportion of unions between men and women begin with an abduction.[16]

The survival of practices of this kind, which would appear at first blush to be so unlikely, suggests, once again, a fragmented economic geography wherein violence plays a central role not just for patrolling social boundaries but also in breaking down communitarian ties.

Blázquez's study explores precisely these issues. Like all of the poppy-growing regions of Mexico (which are erroneously imagined as the point where organized crime originates), Badiraguato is part of a zone wherein difficulty of access has been deliberately made into an economic resource. This resource is mainly exploited by a class of merchant-caciques, known locally as *pesados* (men of weight), who have enough money to finance peasant poppy growers as well as the strength of arms needed to defend their distant ranches and protect the commercialization of their product (opium gum).

Blázquez shows that geographic isolation is a key resource for this dominant class of caciques, who meld financial capital, coercive force, and the networks and ability to negotiate with municipal and state authorities, as well as with the army. Violence is an instrument that serves to build and accentuate the physical remoteness or isolation that poppy-growing peasants and their *pesado* bosses both rely on. Indeed, the region's isolation is the combined result of physical distance and a deliberately cultivated geography of fear that has attached risks to traveling to Badiraguato. Similar strategies of heightening distance by violent means have developed in other drug-producing regions of Mexico, such as Michoacán's Tierra Caliente or the mountains of Guerrero, as well as in a number of urban areas where illicit economies need to interrupt ease of access.

Alongside this politics of isolation, the territories within Badiraguato are fragmented around the boundaries of various hamlets (ranchos). These boundaries are always contentious and subject to invasion and even to the eviction of local communities. The *pesados* and their gunmen have a role in defending those ranchos with which they are identified. In a context like that, stealing women again becomes not only viable, but in fact much more violent than it had been in the Mexican countryside fifty or sixty years ago. Keeping a woman confined in a community is more difficult than it used to be, and neither the women nor the men of those communities have easy recourse to government mediators because they all live off of an illicit economy. As a result, a kind of neotraditional marriage has developed, which is locally referred to as *Ley del Monte* ("Mountain Law" or "Law of the Wild"). Frequently, this sort of marriage is marked by the use of violence in the abduction of women, and it might be thought of as a neo- or pseudo-traditionalist form of marriage that is facilitated by a complex and violently enforced economic geography.

Disappearances

I conclude with a few remarks concerning the forced disappearance of women in today's Mexico. As opposed to the practice of bride theft, the disappearance of women does not lead to the creation of a conjugal tie or a household. Both old-school bride theft and the neotraditional practice as discussed for Badiraguato are stratagems designed to anchor a young woman in a family; the phenomenon of forced disappearance, on the other hand, does not build on social interdependence the way that old-style bride theft did. Rather, disappearance is an act that precedes either murder or enslavement, and so the communitarian relations of the stolen women's families generally become deeply strained, rather than reinforced, with disappearances.

We still have not assimilated the social implications of disappearance, which has reached such tragic proportions today in Mexico, with around 95,000 people disappeared and not found, either alive or dead, according to the official count in November 2021. In practical terms, a disappearance means that there can be no mourning of the victim, and without mourning the line between life and death gets blurred. For this reason, the family members of a disappeared person cannot return to what had until that point been normality.

There are many consequences of a situation of this kind, and all of them affect the social fabric: there are husbands who leave their wives because the wife is a daily reminder of their son's or daughter's disappearance and of the husband's impotence and inability to recover the one abducted. Often, the mother, father, sister, or brother of someone who has been disappeared begins slowly to feel invisible as well. A mother, for instance, may feel that she cannot talk about what she has done during the day (seek out her disappeared loved one, or become submerged in depression, or try to lose herself within her own mind), because the subject of the loved one's absence makes itself unavoidably present in conversation and produces discomfort. Disappearance produces deeply troubling uncertainties—the disappeared person is neither ascertainably alive nor dead—and as such it produces a kind of awkwardness and unease. Friends and acquaintances can neither offer condolences nor easily suggest a change of subject. And so the family members of the disappeared begin to feel like they themselves are disappearing from their dwindling social world, which becomes trite and formal.

The psychosocial effects of this condition, which has now engulfed so many families in Mexico, have still been insufficiently discussed, but we know that the stain associated with disappearance is spreading, and that the interminable suffering associated with it produces concentric circles of silence, holes in human communication that are leaving Mexican society like a Swiss cheese.

The various traditional and neotraditional practices of stealing women that we have reviewed were all geared toward anchoring young women in marriage and toward rooting young couples in a community. The forced disappearance of women, on the other hand, uses violent means to generate expansive holes in families and to leave them suspended in a limbo between life and death. As in the case of Caro Quintero, who was a benefactor in his ranch in Badiraguato and a slaveowner in neighboring Chihuahua, violent social organizations can steal women in order to consolidate families in some instances and steal them in order to destroy families and communities in others. And if we do not make an effort to describe, study, and understand how these contrasting logics relate to the complex geography of illicit economies, we shall fail to comprehend the political dimensions of our contemporary violence.

Conclusion

In this first lecture I have presented the theme with which I shall be occupied during my conference cycle this year, which is the analysis of what we now refer to as Mexico's torn social fabric. I proposed a few elements needed in order to study the matter by focusing on the connection between reciprocity and violence within complex economic geographies.

I argued, first, that today's explosion of violence cannot be understood through any narrative that hinges on a tale of a war on drugs, because drugs are both poison and medicine—and so they can never be eradicated—and because drugs are also thought to be the cause of all crime, so that the people involved in the drug economy easily serve as scapegoats. I argued, too, that our contemporary surge in violence is a symptom of the consolidation of a new type of state, for which we still do not have a name, but that is no longer an instance of a (developing) welfare state, and that can be characterized generally with the formula "Much sovereignty, little administration of justice."

I then laid out a few general ideas concerning the connection between specific kinds of reciprocal relationships and violence, with an emphasis on three points: first, that when group violence goes unchecked and has no negative consequences for its perpetrators, it paves the way for the rise of a caste system; second, that when violence is reciprocal and symmetrical, it careens into a spiral of the sort that can be observed between neighboring urban gangs, for instance; and third, that when there is asymmetry in the deployment of violence, but violent displays are constrained spatially by the action of a weak state, a system of local strongmen—*cacicazgos*—emerges. I argued that it is useful to study how these three forms of negative reciprocity operate and relate, in order to comprehend the connection between illicit economies and the new Mexican state.

My next point was to note that today's illicit economies frequently rely on the articulation of activities that transpire in distant territories, and that this multilocal quality goes hand in hand with a differentiated set of strategies for gaining compliance, particularly regarding the connection between reciprocity and violence. I thus showed why it is that the same bosses who operate as "social bandits" in their home communities can be slavers somewhere else, or simple businessmen in yet other places. And why they can steal a woman to live with her in some contexts, and disappear a woman in order to destroy her family forever in others. In a different sort of example, an urban gang that identifies with its neighborhood can become a predator of that same neighborhood, if it is articulated to a "cartel," and through it, to a transnational economic geography.

I then closed with a few ideas regarding the theft of women and forced disappearance. I showed that bride theft, which had long been part of the traditional repertoire of available strategies leading to marriage in the Mexican countryside, was a strategy that leaned and depended on the "good health" of the social fabric, whereas bride theft in the deliberately isolated territories of today's drug economy implies an intensification of violence inside the community. And I concluded with a few thoughts on the ways in which both traditional and neotraditional forms of bride theft contrast with today's staggering figures of disappearance, noting that whereas bride theft was geared toward rooting women in families and communities, forced disappearance destroys families and weakens their social networks.

The rise of the new state and the geography of the crisis of communitarian mores shall be the subject of my Colegio Nacional lectures this year.

"The State Did It!" (And It Still Does It)

*F**ue el Estado!*" (The state did it!) This was the cry that burst out during the protests that followed the forced disappearance of the forty-three Ayotzinapa students. The accusation is spot on, because there is no doubt that "the state" was responsible both for the disappearances that occurred that night in the city of Iguala and for the procedural nightmare that was—and continues to be—the forensic investigation that followed. The city of Iguala's municipal police force—which was directly involved in the kidnapping of the students—was controlled by the Guerreros Unidos crime organization, and José Luis Abarca, Iguala's municipal president, was the son-in-law and brother-in-law of three drug lords who were on the attorney general's list of Mexico's most dangerous criminals. In other words, the state was both directly and indirectly responsible for the disappearances and assassinations that took place on that day.

There were, moreover, other governmental institutions that were implicated in the crime. So, for instance, the leadership of the Partido de la Revolución Democrática (PRD) had chosen José Luis Abarca as their candidate for the municipal presidency despite his known ties to Iguala's drug economy. It is fair to say that the crime the municipal government perpetrated was made possible thanks either to the negligence or to the connivance of a national political party. The army, for its part, has a military base in Iguala, allegedly with a mission to control opium production in the region, yet it also cultivated a cordial relationship with the municipal government despite its known ties to the Beltrán Leyva drug organization and to a chain of disappearances and assassinations. To all this we must add the incompetence displayed by the attorney general's office around the criminal investigation that followed the disappearances, an incompetence that is at once genuine and contrived, possibly to protect the military from being tarnished by the scandal.

In other words, yes, the state did it. However, although this is true to the letter, the slogan also eludes the political implications of that signal event. Do we really understand the relationship of a municipal government that has been "captured" by a criminal organization with a state government that has to make room for multiple, competing crime organizations, and further, with the federal government and with national political parties? Although it is true that "the state did it," the slogan that purportedly calls out and dares "speak the truth to" power serves instead to veil or conceal a wish—which is expressed as an assertion—that the Mexican state is governed smoothly from top to bottom, from the federal government down to local governments, with an effective administrative division of labor and a clear chain of command with the president at its apex. The case of the Iguala disappearances (killings) is disturbing because it suggests the opposite: this was a crime that was perpetrated by a municipal government that was under the control of a private crime syndicate, with the connivance, we now know, of the local military command, and yet the federal government—represented both by the army and by the justice apparatus—proved to be incapable either of preventing the crime or of doing justice afterward. The criminal state seems, then, to be a facet of an invertebrate state—to recall an expression put forth by José Ortega y Gasset in 1921, in relation to his native Spain[1]—whose parts are not constrained by a chain of command.

▨ My second lecture explores the origin of this new invertebrate state by way of an analysis of how policing functioned before the current era: I will focus on the workings of the police before the recurring attempts at reform were initiated in the mid-1990s, and also before the government finally gave up on its attempts at reform and decided to put public safety in the military's purview. I shall focus specifically on when and how the Mexican state began to become estranged from the mechanisms of police and justice that it had relied on during most of the twentieth century.

The State Estranged from Itself

The state is not a person and it doesn't have a person's sentiments, so in principle it should not be capable of being estranged, either from itself or from anything else. Moreover, from an institutional perspective, the state has never been a vertically integrated structure. What do I mean, then, when I say that we are facing a state that no longer knows itself?

In a paper that is today recognized as a classic, Phillip Abrams sought to reconcile the thinking of Ralph Milliband, who saw the state not as a collective subject but rather as a bundle of institutions and functions that weren't necessarily coordinated or integrated into a single scheme, with the position of Nicos Poulantzas, who viewed the state as a kind of mask, a kind of spectral subject—a false "person" in Marcel Mauss's sense—or, perhaps, as a metaperson, in David Graeber and Marshall Sahlins's terms, which plays the part of the sovereign figure and thus appears to enjoy the autonomy that we associate with the figure of the individual.[2] The state as mask adopts the figure of indivisibility that is implicit in the idea of sovereignty, and so it acquires the attributes of a person, with a will, senses, intelligence, a sense of honor, and so forth.

In the Mexican case, the state as mask is embodied in the figure of the president of the republic, whose role as state fetish is well known. Thus, in his essay on precisely this subject, Juan Espíndola explained how the myth of the president's reputedly omnimodal power was mobilized even by the academics and journalists whose job it was, in principle, to question it: "Only the presidency was subjected to academic and journalistic scrutiny because its imprint was believed to be present everywhere in Mexico's political processes, because its decisions— it was thought—determined the direction that Mexican public life would subsequently follow."[3]

This myth's power of persuasion was rooted in the highly ritualized subservience of politicians and civil servants, who routinely justified their policies and decisions by aligning them with the president's words and sentiments, as well as in the material props of government: photos of the president of the republic hanging in a place of honor in every government office—a monarchical practice that, in Mexico, spilled into the republican era without alteration and suggests that the authority of each institution emanates from the president. In other words, the state is at once a jumble of institutions and the idea that suggests that the sovereignty of the people has been deposited in the person of the president, and so the state assumes the sensitive qualities of a subject, capable of planning, acting, and reacting.

When I speak, then, of the state being estranged from itself, I am referring to two different sorts of situations: one in which the state-as-mask—the sovereign state, which is always personified—seems to be bewildered and takes its distance from governmental operations that had, up until that point, been normal; and the other, in which coordination between state institutions becomes impossible. In this lecture I will focus particularly on cases in which the sovereign state has become estranged from one of its institutions—the police—as well as on cases in which the various institutions that together compose the government's public security apparatus can no longer be reconciled and have lost the capacity to engage reliably in coordinated action.

I will use the term *estrangement* in three senses, two of which are summarized in the French term *méconnaissance*, a term that has the virtue of blending two ideas: ignorance and incomprehension. The third meaning of estrangement comes from the Freudian concept of the uncanny (*unheimlich*), which refers to moments in which the ordinary appears as strange or sinister. For Lacan, this sensation emerges in contexts in which we can no longer distinguish between the good and the bad, or between pleasure and vexation.[4]

I shall focus on the state's estrangement with regard to its institutions of police and justice, concentrating particularly on the police corps known as the *policía preventiva* (preventive police), which constitute the vast majority of Mexico's police forces, and especially on municipal police forces, which are the most visible police organizations and have historically been the most frequent subject of accusations of corruption, indolence, and incompetence. The district attorneys, with their inspectors and the plain-clothes Policía Judicial Federal (Federal Judicial Police) corps that is under their command, are much less visible—except to the poor people who end up in their clutches—while they are also more widely feared. Because they are less visible day-to-day, state estrangement with regard to the Judicial Police tends to crop up sporadically, usually precipitated by scandals that make their incompetence or bad faith public.

My premise is that Mexico's neoliberal transition (1980s–1990s) involuntarily gave way to the formation of a new kind of state, whose operating principles we have not wished to recognize or name and are marked by neglect of the administration of justice and policing, together with the strengthening of state sovereignty, and are manifested in militarization and the concentration of power in the presidency. If, under the modernizing dictatorship of Porfirio Díaz, the operating motto was "Plenty of administration, not a lot of politicking" (*Poca política, mucha administración*), today's state might be tempted to pro-claim its governing philosophy as "Plenty of sovereignty, not a lot of justice."

Estrangement's Beginnings

When did the Mexican state start to become distanced from its own police apparatus? The literature confirms that the topic was hot in the 1990s, when a number of important initiatives were set forth to reform the police.[5] Indeed, by that decade the rush to reform the country's municipal police forces was a theme that all political parties adopted in their electoral campaigns, and that was especially prominent in the moderate right-wing Partido de Acción Nacional (PAN) that held sway in much of the country's north. Police reform became a recurring theme in local and state elections, and since no political party stepped up to defend the police, the country as a whole set itself on the course of reform.

Thus, after his election to the presidency (1995), Ernesto Zedillo commissioned a diagnostic study of the police, which found that public investment in police was ridiculously low (0.008 percent of GDP), and that 56 percent of the preventive police—that is a majority, nationwide—had a sixth-grade education or lower.[6] For starters, and to address this level of apparent "negligence," the police reforms that were initiated in the mid-1990s began by pumping a (proportionally) enormous amount of money into security so that, by 2009, budgets for police accounted for 1.7 percent of GDP, that is, an almost two-hundred-fold increase over what they had been in the prereform era.

Those moneys were channeled into improving the policemen's working conditions—salary increases, new benefits, housing programs, retirement funds—as well as training, armament, equipment, uniforms, and the creation of an institutional framework that might be used to build a professional, capable police. Both the improvement of working conditions and investments in training and equipment had the following objectives: to eliminate the policemen's economic dependence on corruption, to make the police force more competent and effective, to train it to respect human rights, and to "dignify" policemen—that is, to elevate their social status—in order thereby to foster a collaborative, supportive relationship between citizens and the police.

It is clear that such an expensive, sweeping process of reform would not have been undertaken had there not been widespread repudiation of the police, far beyond the sort of mild-to-moderate dissatisfaction we might find today with regard to, say, Mexico's mediocre and underperforming educational system. No one stepped up to defend the police.

Even so, reforms on this scale are often sparked by specific events and, indeed, there were two developments that got the ball of reform rolling. The first was a public scandal around the doings of Arturo a.k.a. "El Negro" Durazo, who served as Mexico City's chief of police during the government of José López Portillo (1976–82), and whose doings were detailed in an exposé, published in 1983, just months after the collapse of the Mexican peso that led to the country's first steps toward neoliberal reform. The second factor was a series of crime waves that stormed Mexico City and some other important towns, which had peaks in the years 1984–85, 1987, 1993, and 1995.

These two instigating factors suggest distinct and contrasting dynamics leading up to the estrangement of the Mexican state with regard to the modus operandi of its police. The first factor, provoked by the publication of *Lo negro del Negro Durazo* (The dark side of "El Negro" Durazo)—a book that so enthralled the public that it then gave way to the production of comic books (see figure 2.1), films, and an endless stream of comments—suggests the role of a dynamic that was tied to regime change. The Miguel de la Madrid government began in January 1983 under the cloud of the worst economic crisis that Mexico had faced in generations. This led to a change in the country's guiding economic orientation, from import substitution industrialization (building up domestic industry to cut reliance on imports) to neoliberalism. In such a deep crisis, the image of a cynical and inefficient police force, corrupt top to bottom, became emblematic of the wasteful, iniquitous disorder of the previous regime, which had gotten Mexico into such a deep rut, and which now had to be paid for by the entire citizenry with severe penury. The corruption of the police under the prior regime was thus mobilized to help legitimate the new president, whose campaign motto had been "The Moral Renovation of Society," and who had to slash budgets in a contracting economy that was prey to hyperinflation.

The preventive police—those police corps that we see daily in uniform, and whose incompetence and corruption is also in plain sight—was revealed as an institution that undermined society's most precious values: it raped and prostituted women; it had insinuated itself in the corrupt world of elite homosexuals; it blackmailed, extorted, murdered, and robbed so much that even criminals began to complain about it. So, for instance,

Figure 2.1. From *El infierno del Negro Durazo* [The inferno of "El Negro" Durazo], ca. 1983. Top panel: (*caption*) We shall not repeat the ignominy of the past: so much sadism, such haughtiness, so much ambition. All of Mexico demands this. [*man speaking into mic [President Miguel de la Madrid]*] "All abuses of authority should be prohibited: torture as a method of investigation, and the collusion between policemen and delinquents . . ." [*man in glasses*] We should not remain silent, we need to demand justice now that there is a moralizing wind brought by President Miguel de la Madrid. Bottom panel: (*caption*) For Mexico to be able to eradicate all forms of immorality, it must fight alongside its president. (*banner*) Death to [Co]rruption.

José González González, author of the book that gave rise to the public's morbid fascination with the dirty deeds of police chief Durazo, introduced himself in its first pages as a professional hit man, who had murdered more than fifty people, following the orders of ex-presidents, members of the cabinet, and other first-tier political figures. But he had, nonetheless, taken "the decision to risk my well-being for an ideal, which is to come clean with the public opinion of my country in these times when Mexico has been subjected to ruthless and antipatriotic looting by haughty, abusive, and pilfering politicians. We hitmen also love Mexico in our way."[7]

The government that now distanced itself from that infamous police force sought to highlight a distinction between the wastefulness and corruption of the López Portillo presidency and the austere morality of President De la Madrid and, at a deeper level, between a corporatist, protectionist petrostate and an austere, fiscally responsible, neoliberal state. The state's estrangement from the police was, in this regard, part of a political movement.

The second factor that led to state estrangement vis-à-vis its police force was a set of shocking crime waves that hit Mexico City in the 1980s and 1990s and that marked the beginnings of something like an "industrial revolution" of crime in the country.

Unfortunately, we do not yet have a detailed study of these crime waves, but there is information that helps us at least to sketch out some general features. First, these waves of ordinary crime (muggings, break-ins, kidnappings) signaled the end of an era during which crime had remained pretty stable. Legal scholar Ana Laura Magaloni shows that reported crimes in Mexico City had diminished considerably between 1940 and 1960, and that they had remained stable between 1960 and 1980. Then, starting in 1983, after forty years of comparative security, crime began to mount until it reached its highest peak in a terrible crime wave in the mid-1990s.[8] In a matter of just a few years, Mexico City went from being a relatively safe city to being very unsafe.[9]

Moreover, the crimes of the 1980s and 1990s involved unusual displays of violence. Victims were beaten and terrorized, insulted, verbally assaulted, and threatened with guns. Occasionally, muggers killed their victims. This sort of violence had been exceptional until then. So, for example, film director Everardo González produced a documentary titled *Los ladrones viejos* (The old thieves), in 2007, in which he interviewed pickpockets and burglars being held in Mexico City's Santa Martha Acatitla prison. Those burglars had operated in Mexico City during the 1950s to 1970s, and listening to them infuses one with genuine nostalgia for yesteryear's holdups, carried out by true professionals who knew how to do their thieving without hurting or threatening their victims: their art consisted of acting without being noticed. The crime of the 1980s and 1990s was something else entirely.

We still don't know the reasons for this change, or whether there is a technological backdrop to it—the proliferation of guns, automobiles, and motorbikes, for instance, or the invention of cellular phones. Nor do we know whether the depth of the economic crisis of the 1980s and 1990s was a factor, or even whether the measures taken after the Durazo scandal frayed the police force's tacit agreements with the criminal world and thus disincentivized police interventions that had regulated criminal violence in the past.

We do know, however, that Mexican society began to resent insecurity. And, further, that the ineffective policy responses to this new insecurity only deepened the state's estrangement with regard to the police, to such an extent that, little by little, the government shifted from a politics of distancing itself from the old system of policing to the expression of frustration and impotence in the face of its sustained failure to bring security back. The reforms of the 1990s demonstrated that the state— represented in both its executive and legislative branches— didn't have a firm grasp on how its own police forces functioned, and over time their consistently lackluster results provoked further estrangement between the state as sovereign and the state as institutions for administering police.

The Work of the Police

One of the main problems of the reformist movement was its proclivity to ignore the order that was produced by everyday policework. Dissatisfaction and repugnance with the police was amply justified and widely felt, but it led reformists to focus on police abuse and inefficacy without looking closely at the police's work in the construction of a social order. The proliferation of criminals within the various police corps, their lack of professional training and low educational level, the corruption that was endemic to the police as an institution, its minimal capabilities in forensics, the general paucity of inspired leadership, and the police's routine human rights abuses dominated the reformers' attention, and they then tried to mitigate or extirpate these and other horrors. A great deal of effort went into improving the police force's working conditions—especially salaries and benefits—with the theory that corruption was a result of low wages. New police academies opened, as well as specialized police units, and higher educational standards were now required for entry. Human rights were introduced as an indispensable dimension of police work. There were also substantial investments in armament and other policing equipment. The image of the humble policeman, on foot with his bobby stick and perhaps a pistol, gave way to police bearing automatic weapons and body armor atop shiny new motorcycles, patrol cars, and four-by-fours. Some of these measures were laudable, but little attention was placed on the relationship between police abuse and the role of the police as an instrument of social and economic regulation.

I offer some examples of this, in order to explain what I mean.

When a policeman caught a thief, it was common practice to beat the culprit, take his belongings (sometimes even his shoes), and for the police who caught him to keep not only the thief's personal effects but also his loot. In the eyes of the reformer, there were two big problems with this mode of operation: first, the fact that the policemen took it upon themselves to punish suspects directly by beating them and taking their property, which implied that the police, who were supposed to be "preventive," had in fact usurped the roles of the judge and of the penal institutions; and second, that the police kept the loot, instead of returning it to its rightful owner. Both of these problems occupied reformers, while they paid less attention to the nature of the system of crime regulation that was in place. Mexican police were practically useless when it came to doing justice to victims of robbery (except in cases where the victim had a lot of political pull) and, as a result, they also did not reduce the amounts taken in any given robbery. Indeed, because the police kept the loot, they tended to prefer it if the thief had stolen a lot. But, as abusive as they were, those police practices did inhibit stealing to some degree: given their role as the thief's thief, policemen had some material incentives to catch thieves. Reformers were bent on reducing police corruption by way of improving salaries and benefits and introducing higher standards of professionalism but, by taking their regular operating procedures from the police, they turned their back on the meager but real regulating effects of the police force's rudimentary procedures. Reformers saw the "rot" in police practices with some clarity but ignored the "positive" effects that they had in reproducing an unjust but nonetheless well-established and operational social order.

A second sort of situation had bigger consequences. Police reformers worried about a subculture of secrecy and complicity in the police. One of the first lessons that academy cadets were taught was not to rat out their fellow officers, nor should they convey information regarding the names or identifiable markers of officers involved in any particular operation. As one policeman put it: "No se chivatea sobre lo que se habla y se escucha; no hay nombres ni características de compañeros ni comandantes" (We don't rat out on anything that colleagues say, nor do we share information on the names or description of fellow cops or commanding officers).[10] In order to reform the police and modernize their practices, honest policemen would need to be able to come forward with accusations against their corrupt colleagues; it would also be necessary to fire corrupt or inept policemen, correct selection criteria, reform police training in the academies, and introduce new, honest, and professional police captains. The silence and complicity among policemen—their identity as a kind of mafia—was always one of the hurdles for reform. However, again, the reformers did not give proper attention to the full effects of the practice that they sought to root out, because the fact that the various police corps operated as mafias also gave them strength with regard to other, competing mafias, and the police began to be weakened as they started to be divided between "corrupt" and "honest" members. In order to understand this aspect of the problem, we offer a few considerations about the police force's role in the regulation of the informal economy.

44

Police and the Regulation of Informality

The relatively few ethnographic studies that we have of Mexico's police suggest that, at least until the time of the reforms, the police were capable of functioning like a criminal organization. Police corps often included a certain number of officers who had prior connections to the criminal world—they were assets that came in handy when the police were negotiating deals with criminals. In addition, a high percentage of recruits did not have enough formal education to get placed above the poorest in the labor market, and there were significant numbers of violent recruits, often with serious psychological problems.

In a field study of a municipal police corps published in 1998, the sociologists Nelson Arteaga and Adrián López describe the entry process of a police academy. They begin by noting that candidates did not register as lone individuals, but rather they always came in small groups of acquaintances from the same neighborhood. Even before enrolling in the police academy, the majority of the aspiring candidates "integrate in groups where conversation flows with natural familiarity, they smoke from the same cigarette and share soft drinks from the same bottle."[11]

Corporations are in fact made up of small groups of family members or neighbors. Indeed, the decision to try out for the police academy tended to happen only after an informal process of recruiting, so our authors explain that "entry to the Municipal police depends on previously existing relationships with people who are already in the service." In other words, a prior personal connection between recruits and servicemen was at times a precondition for admission. On the other hand, the ubiquity of bribery in the process of selection and training also produced cohesion, because candidates knew beforehand—precisely thanks to the lore that was passed on to them by friends who were in the service—that the selection process involved making a (substantial) investment that would be recouped once the candidate was a policeman. The constant bribes that recruits paid in their training in the police academy were, in part, a rite of passage to their entry to an economy that relied crucially on bribes. In this sense, bribery was a practice that led to police cohesion. Candidates knowingly sought entry into a corrupt order, this order had its established hierarchies and precepts, and the aspiring policemen needed to be introduced to those.

The case described by Arteaga and López—whose possible representativeness I shall discuss later—offers a few other revealing details as well. The three main exams that trainees needed to pass—the psychological examination, the academic test, and the general fitness test—could all be passed with bribes, and all candidates knew this before enrolling. At the same time, those examinations had a pedagogical side that is quite jarring, which is their arbitrariness and—in many cases— their apparent lack of relevance. The psychological tests seem to have been incomprehensible even for those who administered them, and who, by the way, were often not qualified to interpret them. Thus, in her study of a police academy in Guadajalara in the 1990s—which was an institution that was a bit less rotten than the one described by Arteaga and López— anthropologist María Eugenia Suárez de Garay cites the opinion of the psychologist in charge of administering the test: "I think that these medical-psychological exams were designed for Martians. They don't seem to fit the classical Mexican. We Mexicans are totally different from any other race.... I would strongly question the validity of the psycho-biological exam, the test of the mind."[12] The psychological tests did not get better ratings from those who took them, either: "They give us a psychological test when we enter the academy, but it is so poor! I'm not a psychologist, but it's an exam where you say to yourself: 'This test can't tell you whether a policeman will bear up to the pressure of the job, or whether he has some sort of trauma or perversion (*desviación*)."[13]

Even the physical fitness exams, which are obviously pertinent for the job, were frequently applied in such an arbitrary manner that their actual bearing on candidates' suitability was doubtful. The candidates studied by Arteaga and López had to pass a test consisting of doing a very long run with no prior training; the majority of them ended up hitching rides or taking public transportation to reach the finish line. Neither did the academy offer a serious program to build fitness so that, although the academy touted the pertinence of physical training, it was not sufficiently interested in the matter to invest in the necessary training facilities.

But the academic exams were perhaps the most telling, because they reflected the relationship between the police and the laws they were meant to uphold. Before the reforms—and this may well be still valid today—Mexican police lived off of transgressions of the law. Their mission was not to be the stewards of the spirit of the law, but rather to gain their livelihood from any and all infractions to the letter of the law. For this reason, Mexican police have always been fond of useless rules, the more abstruse, the better. The more a rule is illogical or counterintuitive, the more it will be violated, and the more money it will bring into the policeman's pocket. Policemen are thus instruments of the law not as "servants of the public"—not as employees whose salaries are paid for by the citizenry—but rather as vigilantes who have permission to take money from anyone who breaks the law. From the viewpoint of the police, the law is not there to be either just or fair, it is simply there. The law is an arbitrary fact. And, seen from this angle, the academic exams that cadets were presented with did indeed offer some sort of lesson.

Arteaga and López enumerate the questions in those exams. Some communicated a structure of authority: What day of the year is the president's State of the Union address? What is the meaning of the acronym PRI? Which are the three symbols of the nation? Others were so ambiguous that they served only to underline the fact that only the teacher knows the right answer: What is a policeman? What is a regulation? Finally, there were yet other questions—meant to test for general knowledge—that were absolutely arbitrary: In which voyage did Columbus discover America? What is the capital of Singapore? When was the first printing press installed in Mexico? What did the process for extracting silver that the Spaniards implemented after the Conquest consist of? The academic exams thus transmitted a structure of authority and exemplified that authority's arbitrariness and the ultimate irrelevance of the specific contents of the law.

A third revealing detail from Arteaga and López's ethnography is that, after they had concluded their training and exams, while they were waiting for the admissions results to be posted, the aspiring trainees took a minute to gather in a secluded spot, behind the police academy, to smoke a joint. Arteaga and López remark that "the consumption and distribution of weed throughout the entire training program allowed the small groups that had existed at the beginning to fuse into a large group that now arranged itself in a circle, with the joint circulating from right to left."

There is nothing remarkable about these cadets developing a ritual to mark the end of their training, but it is interesting that, instead of alcohol, they preferred to use marijuana as the medium for bonding; the "host" that they chose for their communion is an illegal substance the use of which, at the time of the study, was a punishable offense that could land users in prison for several years. Their choice of substance was thus not trivial.

The marijuana that united these cadets was symbolically powerful, because the police had the prerogative of smoking it without taking a risk, and because it is an example of the kind of substance that would later bring them their sustenance, precisely because it was illegal. Since the police force in Mexico accomplished its regulatory functions by extracting bribes from those who broke the law, the police lived, in a strict sense, off of illegal acts. Indeed, it was strictly true that the police lived off of illegal acts as much as the criminal did. Legal infractions were, then, the policeman's livelihood: for a policeman, a "good corner" was a corner where there are lots of traffic violations, not a sleepy one where there were none; a lucrative neighborhood was one where there were plenty of bars without liquor licenses, where there was illegal street prostitution, and plenty of street vendors and informal stalls. Illegal activity ended up constituting a policeman's potential wealth, for he would keep a portion of the thief's loot, receive free sex and take money from illegal prostitutes, consume and resell drugs taken from addicts, and take free meals from informal vendors. The fact that pot was smoked at the communion ritual that the cadets invented as a kind of informal graduation ceremony recognized the place of illegal activities and substances in their future livelihood.

It is worth asking whether these conclusions—garnered from a few ethnographies—are generalizable for all police corporations of the prereform era. The question is not trivial. One of the characteristics of Mexican state and municipal police corps—which was a real headache for reformers, too—was their great number and diversity. In the 1990s, there were more than 1,600 police forces in Mexico.[14] Each force had to adjust its work to divergent circumstances, so that no one characterization suits all cases. The police corps of a rural municipality, with three officers on its payroll who had perhaps been handpicked for the job by the local cacique, could not be the same as the corps that operated in a city, with two hundred, five hundred, or even thousands of officers. A municipal force with three officers could not constitute itself as the kind of quasi-criminal organization described by Arteaga and López because, in the rural setting, the policeman had to negotiate any legal infraction from a position of numerical vulnerability and of dependency on and deep social ties to the villagers among whom he lived.

In general terms, it still seems useful to distinguish between police corps that are embedded in their communities and inevitably small in size, and the medium and large police organizations capable of routine engagement in an extractive set of practices. On the other hand, within urban contexts, a precinct that operates in a neighborhood that has plenty of conflict and plenty of formal and informal businesses will not operate in the same way as a precinct that sits in the center of a quiet middle-class residential neighborhood.

This diversity might also explain some of the differences—or at least different shades of a similar reality—that can be gleaned from various case studies. So, for instance, Suárez de Garay found that in Guadalajara "The policemen and women appreciated what they learned in the academy, which was perhaps the most real training that most of them ever got in any educational institution—and many expressed noble sentiments regarding what the police is and what they aspire to, even though they are conscious about matters of corruption, etc."[15]

This finding contrasts with the hardened cynicism described by Arteaga and López in "their" academy, true, but the sentiments don't really say what those noble Guadalajara cadets would actually be doing once they were out on the streets. They themselves recognized that the training that they received in the academy—which was better than what they got in elementary school (their average educational level)—was not only insufficient, and frequently outright inadequate, but also "theoretical." Indeed, the consensus among Suárez's interviewees was that "the street is the best teacher." Teacher of what? It is the teacher of which infringements and violations they will be living off of, and which they shall, therefore, be involved in regulating.

On the other hand, despite significant differences in police practices—all of which are in fact learned "on the streets" and are related to the size of each police corps and to the specific form of imbrication that each police force has in its community of operation—when the state felt that it was time to reform the police, it sought to streamline, rationalize, and centralize as a governing strategy. Its aim was that Mexico's hundreds of police forces might be consolidated as either state or federal police, and that the police as a whole might pass from being identified as adjacent to crime to being perceived as firmly in the command of the state. This policy meant concentrating power—specifically, wrenching autonomy away from municipal police forces and placing all meaningful authority in the hands of state and federal police. Frequently this drive to centralize police authority also involved militarizing the chain of command, a policy that increased the illusion or conceit of federal control over policing.

One immediate effect of these policies was that small police corps were further debilitated, and policing was increasingly commandeered either from the governor's office or from the presidency. This policy seems to have backfired with regard to its ultimate effects on security.

Chain of Command and Money

I have so far argued that the preventive police—state or municipal—can be thought of as something akin to criminal organizations with a patent, a bit like pirates in the Elizabethan era, whose licensed targets were breakers of the law who were then shaken down for money and other resources. It was this patent or license that differentiated the police from other bands of extortionists, because belonging to the police required a formal appointment, and it involved receiving a salary, a uniform (although sometimes the policemen were expected to buy their own uniforms), a gun (ditto), and other equipment (also, ditto), since these were all necessary to make it clear to everyone that these were employees and representatives of the Mexican state. Although the salaries, arms, uniforms, and equipment were insufficient for the police to do their job, and although these official resources needed to be supplemented with income acquired through bribery and extortion, the fact that these were public employees, who could also be fired, demoted, relocated, or even prosecuted for dereliction of duty, allowed for the existence of an impersonal chain of command. Indeed, one of the lessons that a new policeman was taught by his training officer was, "Don't argue with the chiefs, officers in charge, or any officer or senior fellow officer, because the higher-ups are always right."[16] In other words, the police force is different from other criminal organizations because it is a bureaucratic structure.

However, the Mexican police were not a modern bureaucracy, but rather a hybrid social organization form between a modern bureaucracy and an ancién régime prebendal mode of administration, where government posts are bought and sold, and the purchase of a post is a license for its use for personal gain. This hybrid form has implications that, again, distinguish the police from the criminals who operate extortion or protection rackets.

Perhaps the most revealing difference between these two social organizational forms was the use of money inside police corporations. So, for instance, a trainee who was closely studied by Arteaga and López heard the following dictum from his training officer: "Everything in the corporation involves money. No favor to fellow police or to commanders or higher-ups is done out of good will. Everything needs to be paid for." Money thus operated in the police force as a universal equivalent that was used to streamline the flow of income, since the police dealt systematically with two revenue sources, one that came from the official budget, and the other that emanated from the entrepreneurial activities of individual officers.

Monetary exchanges between policemen were used to assign a price for each task that was done on the job. Because, as the patrolman explained to his trainee, "We don't work here just for work's sake: you will help only those who pay for the service."[17] This maxim suggested that, in theory at least, any task performed by a policeman should be paid for; otherwise it would be a "favor" ("work for work's sake"). Monetary transactions inside the police sought to reduce favors to as close to zero as possible, by assigning a price to each task. This monetizing effort was, in fact, indispensable, and it was independent of the morality of the individual policeman—it was not "corruption" in this sense. Here's why:

The police force had two sources of income: the one that came to it from municipal, state, or federal budgets, and the one that stemmed from the business of protection and from the use of infractions of the law as opportunities for extortion. The police force could not influence or alter the moneys that were assigned to it in government budgets, which were decided on by legislative branches of government, with salaries that were bureaucratically determined. On the other hand, the moneys that came from protection, bribery, and extortion were highly variable, as they were reaped in different kinds of contexts and situations. Often these moneys were extracted by officers on the street (which, by the way, also explains why policemen were so devoted to the mystique of "the street as the best teacher").

The variability of moneys that could be gleaned on the streets allowed for significant income disparities between officers of the same rank, and it even opened up the possibility of having street cops earning more than their bosses. After all, a cop that caught a jewelry thief would keep the loot; while his colleague, of identical rank, passed his day directing traffic with a whistle in his mouth; and his boss kept cashing in the same salary, month after month. Given such disparities, it was important to have a system of resource redistribution within the police force, imperfect though it might have been. And the monetization of tasks was the key to this redistribution.

The system that Mexico's police forces created relied on two different customs. The first was the re-collection of moneys that flowed daily from beat cops to their commanders. This rent is still known as *el entre*, a term that suggests that it is money that needs to be put on the table in order to continue to play, like the ante in a game of poker, and it must be paid religiously. Indeed, the first thing that a beat cop did in his or her patrol was to gather rents from the businesses that purchased police protection—it was from those rents that the policeman paid his own rent—his *entre*—to his superiors. The last act in each day of all street cops was to turn the *entre* over to their superior officer.

The second distributive mechanism devised by this policing method involved the payments that had to be made in exchange for any "favor" received. So, for instance, being assigned a profitable street corner was a favor that required a payment. Receiving backup from another officer in order to catch a jewelry thief was another favor, and so the loot from that sting needed to be divided with him. Passing entrance exams was a favor that needed to be paid for. Changing partners, changing work schedules, getting access to a motorcycle or a patrol car—all of these had a price tag.

It is worth dwelling a bit on some of the effects of these practices. We've already said that monetization of all "favors" allowed for streamlining flows of income within the police hierarchy, so that officers could skim the earnings that street cops gleaned from the everyday milking of violations of law. Indeed, the monetization of all police tasks is what allowed the hybrid structure that combined a rational-bureaucratic social organizational form and an entrepreneurial protection racket to exist.

Monetization of tasks and the institution of rents also reinforced the chain of command, because just as the beat cop had to give up the stable rents that he collected at the end of each working day, so too was he expected to acknowledge that "officers are always right." In this way, police placed limits on the kind of charismatic authority that characterizes criminal organizations, and favored instead an impersonal chain of command and, through it, a degree of political control over the police from outside the corporation. In principle, policemen were free to exploit for their own benefit any infraction of the law that occured within their beat, provided that they paid their rents and any and all favors garnered from other officers, but if they received orders mandating anything that was contrary to their immediate interests, those orders had to be followed, on pain of getting disbarred or thrown in jail.

Given all of this, it is interesting to note that the term *favor* still prevailed within the police, despite the monetization of every administrative or practical task. The persistence of the language of the gift underlined the fact that the police force's bureaucratic organization was not sufficiently strong to induce any specific employee to act. So, for instance, it might be true that a captain has the obligation to assign patrol cars to his officers, but he is not compelled to assign them to any officer in particular, which is why every patrol assignment could be construed as a favor, and that favor would then be repaid, in cash.

If I'm a policeman and I organized a sting to rope in a jewelry thief and you're a patrol officer who supported the sting, you did me a favor, because you could have chosen not to come to the aid of my operation and might have chosen instead to tend to any other "obligation." So, in exchange for that *favor*, I then must decide what proportion of the loot you've earned. The persistence of this rhetoric of exchanges of favors in a system that was, at the same time, so punctiliously monetized was a reflection, again, of the hybrid social organizational form that was the Mexican police, a hybrid that, as I said, was at once a publicly funded bureaucracy and a privatized, entrepreneurial organization.

Two Kinds of Policemen, and the Matter of the "Honest Cop"

This organizational logic produced as its consequence two poles toward which any one policeman gravitated: one of them is conservative and the other is predatory. These gravitational poles reduced the margins of operation of any fresh, idealistic recruit of the sort that our reformists pinned their hopes on— as if the characteristics of our police were a subjective matter.

The golden rule of the policeman that gravitated toward what I'm calling the "conservative" pole is summarized in a popular police maxim: "If you want one day to be an old cop, play dumb and look the other way" (*Si quieres llegar a ser policía viejo, hazte pendejo*). One of the Guadalajara policemen interviewed by Suárez de Garay portrayed this sort of cop in the following terms: "Those are the sort of short, fat, lazy cops [*chaparros, panzones y huevones*] that if anything [bad] is happening, they won't come out and support you."[18] The policemen who gravitated to this conservative pole were less aggressive, less exploitative, and less violent than the ones who tended to the opposite pole, which I'm calling "predatory," but, detrimentally, they were also passive—often to the point of indolence. Arteaga and López described the daily patrol of a team that was led by an officer of this indolent or "conservative" type, whom they call Mario:

> They then came upon two individuals fighting outside a bar, but the policeman ignored them. On the main avenue of that zone they saw two soldiers drinking beer in the street and having a loud argument. The policemen passed them by. While driving on a secondary artery they received a report that two guys were holding up a hair salon. The policeman did not respond to the call. Around eight at night a woman approached them in torn clothes reporting that her husband had beaten her. The policeman ignored her too. Around nine at night, a taxi driver reported that he'd been robbed. The policeman said to his partner: If they mugged him it's because he's a fool (*por pendejo*). At eleven at night the patrolman took a snooze.[19]

The opposite sort of cop, of the predatory type, was interested in making as much money and in getting as many daily benefits as possible, and for this reason he was much less passive than the conservative type. In a day of patrolling like the one we just described for Mario, the predatory cop would have stopped the fight outside the bar—taking some personal risks, perhaps—and he would have gotten money from the brawling parties in exchange for not taking them into the station; he would have tried to catch the guys who were robbing the hair salon and would have kept all or most of what they'd stolen; he would have heeded the beaten woman in order to give her husband a scare, and extort him (and, perhaps, her as well); he would not have intervened in the soldiers' argument, because they belong to another corporation, nor would he have responded to the taxi driver's call for help, because he'd already been robbed and the thief had already left.

Many reformists imagine that between these two types of policemen lives the unicorn that they have always been looking for: the honest cop. And, in fact, there actually were some honest people who opted for a policing career. However, once they entered the corporation, their ability to perform that honesty was restricted since they had to guarantee the daily delivery of the rent (*entre*) to their superiors, which meant charging informal and some formal businesses for protection. If they wanted to be promoted or given any particular job, they had to pay their superiors money for the "favor"; and if they expected to get any assistance from other policemen, they had to offer some remuneration in exchange. Finally, if our unicorn decided to report the misdeeds of any colleague or officer, he or she would be violating the precept of "not ratting out" that was and still is a cardinal principle for the corporation, and would then need to face the consequences.

Suárez de Garay's study—which was undertaken during years of intense reform in the 1990s, when human rights were being introduced to police practice—reports the feeling of isolation and loneliness that was common among newly recruited police officers, who "fear[ed] taking risks, not only in routine policing activities but also in interpersonal relationships, that might end up leaving them unprotected, especially because of the combination of the logic of (dis)loyalty and labor insecurity."[20] The consequences of this feeling of isolation, compounded by the complicity that comes hand in glove with silence and with the need to collaborate and follow certain rules, lead the newly recruited officers to lean either toward the conservative or the predatory pole.

What the Police Force Used to Do

These considerations allow us, finally, to consider what it is the police did before the reforms, and before the crime waves of the 1980s and 1990s. The "passive" policeman was a figure who tended mainly to the rents or to bribes that were very easy to secure. "Mario" thus explained the daily routine to his newly assigned trainee. The first thing in the day was to "collect the rents": "The rents," Mario explained, "are the way in which the police force charges people who sell beer, *pulque* [an alcoholic drink], or wine without a permit. It is the way that the police force gets money in exchange for offering security to the stores, liquor vendors, bars, *pulquerías*, butchers, hair salons, etc. It is an agreement between the store owners and the police." He then explained that these rents went along with a responsibility: "We don't do work for its own sake: you will help the businesses that pay for the service, let those that don't cooperate go to hell."[21]

The minimum of work that a policeman did, then, was to offer protection to the stores and street stalls that paid the police rent, and to make the physical presence of the police in the territory felt by way of making daily rounds. These daily rounds served to create a visible presence, which was and still is also one of the primary functions of the police, since police presence offers viable means to pull the state in as an ally when a person faces a violation of the law. Police presence in public space opens a possible line of state intermediation in social conflict.

On the other hand, the existence of a group of policemen of the predatory type enforced the police's role as inhibitor of rule breaking, because disorder is the space that the predatory policeman relied on for his extortions. Thus, the officer explained to his trainee: "Never hesitate when anything seems suspicious to you, because it *is* suspicious for sure; forge ahead to intervene: it means money."[22]

Police interference in the face of suspicious activity could sometimes be quite violent, in order to dissuade civilians from making any objection or to punish them outright, or, sometimes, for the sheer pleasure of scaring people. Indeed, there is evidence that the routine use of violence was a factor of self-selection for some policemen. For example, security expert Ernesto López-Portillo cites an evaluation of 15,708 policemen, carried out by the Centro Nacional de Educación Superior (CENEVAL) in 2004 and 2005, which found that only 33 percent of police officers had psychological traits that were compatible with a calm and responsible performance of their duties; 22 percent were recommended for preventive therapy and 35 percent for a deep psychological evaluation and/or continuous therapy.[23]

The new recruit whom Arteaga and López followed in his daily rounds ended up gravitating toward the predatory pole, so he paid his superior officers money to be reassigned, and he abandoned our passive and conservative Mario, to become the trainee of "Ricardo," who, after collecting the daily rents (which had been Mario's main activity), patrolled the neighborhood "in search of drunks and drug addicts, who were then detained with shouts and blows to their legs—he robbed them of all of their belongings." He also extorted prostitutes and homosexuals, took drugs from users and some dealers and then sold them on the side ... all of this with frequent displays of violence."[24]

On the other hand, even our indolent Mario was not above using violence when it suited him. He thus explained to his trainee what needed to be done if a bar owner stopped paying rent as follows: "If they do that they can be harassed in their businesses, and in the case of bars that resist payments, the police can go in and rape their prostitutes. As you will see, everything in this trade requires reciprocity."[25]

In sum, the order produced by the police can be characterized in the following manner: first, it created a sharp distinction between protected and unprotected businesses; second, it inhibited public displays that might appear to break the law, since any suspicious act attracted police attention and led to police extortion; third, it established the presence of the state in public space and positioned it as a potential mediator in relations of conflict. For example, had the woman who complained to Mario about her violent husband had the (good or bad) fortune of having taken that same accusation to Ricardo, her husband would have paid heavily for his abuses. The presence of the police in public space was thus a resource that social actors could try to harness in order to defeat others: a store owner who paid rent could sic the police on a street vendor who placed his stall nearby, for instance. The public presence of the police placed the state in a position not of an impartial judge but rather of a potential ally to one or other party in a conflict; an ally who was interested in the production of an order that inevitably benefited some, to the detriment of others.

One of the most common mistakes in popular and media images of the police force in the heyday of reform, in the 1990s and 2000s, was that the police didn't do anything—or that if they did, it only got in the way of things. It was certainly true that many police methods were identical both in form and intent to those of the common thief. However, the old police force did produce an order, through the combination of bureaucratic-political regulation—manifested in the payment of tribute to superior officers (*entres*), as well as in the maxim that "the brass is always right"—and in the fact that extortion consistently used transgressions of the law as its pretext and point of reference. In addition, the police force was commonly used by society as an instrument with which to resolve its own conflicts. The order that resulted was certainly unjust—but it had a social value, and so the police could not be robbed of their modus operandi without other violent actors filling the void.

Conclusion

In the first lecture in this series, on the tear in the social fabric, I proposed the idea that Mexico is witnessing the birth of a new kind of state, characterized by a lot of sovereignty and a diminished ability to administer justice. More precisely, there is a lot of investment in sovereignty paired with the neglect of the state's ability to regulate violence as an everyday factor in the production of order and disorder. This transformation of the state has involved the intensification of the processes that I characterized in this second lecture as the state's estrangement from itself and, in particular, its estrangement from its police apparatus. I located the origin of this process of estrangement in a regime change that began in the early 1980s and in the loss of control over common crime—the crime waves that also began in the 1980s but scaled up dramatically in the 1990s, and whose causes we still ignore.

From there, we moved toward an analysis of the way that the police worked in the era immediately prior to the one that is now developing. I showed that the police force that the reformers of the 1990s and 2000s were trying to change was a hybrid social organizational form that combined principles of modern bureaucracy with a system of private entrepreneurship. Each policeman could operate as an independent agent, though with limits that were set by what I characterized as a kind of license to rob, akin to the sort of patent that the British crown once offered to pirates, so long as they operated against enemies of the state. Each officer's labor conditions were delimited by parameters dictated by a chain of command that routinely weighed monetary considerations against political considerations. For this reason, the old Mexican police worked in an economy in which every task was *at once a favor and a monetary transaction*, or in other words, a political act (a favor) and a commodity (a monetary transaction).

This system had the important quality of coming very cheap to the Mexican state, since the majority of the police force's operating costs were paid for directly by society, by way of bribes and extortions, thanks to the entrepreneurial actions of all policemen. For this reason, too, the police force as a corporation was characterized by rampant abuse of the lower rungs by their superiors. Since governmental budgets for the police represented only the smaller part of the corporations' earnings, authorities had relatively few material incentives to offer their subordinates in order to regulate their work, and this made the abuse of authority into a routinely used resource for the chain of command.

When Mexican governments decided that they wanted to reform this system, they thought that the key problem they needed to solve was the policemen's poor salaries, their poor professional training and, more generally, insufficient public investment in security. Reformists also had the idea that they could purge the forces of their most violent and corrupt officers and substitute them with honest and better trained officers. This strategy had some virtues, certainly, but it soon butted against a reality that it found incomprehensible: insecurity and violence kept increasing despite an enormous jump in public spending.

We still do not have a detailed study that explains the rise in criminality and especially in criminal violence that began in the 1990s, and there were undoubtedly many factors that contributed to it. We shall inspect some of those in my next lecture, but my present remarks have identified at least one of them, which is the lack of attention that reformers paid to the— unjust, violent, and corrupt, certainly, but also real—role that police played in regulating the social order.

In the face of the political pressure that insecurity generated, and without finding a key that allowed them to transform

Mexico's hundreds of police departments into a modern and professional apparatus, the Mexican state moved from its initial distancing to deep estrangement from its police, and from there to the almost total neglect of municipal and preventive policing in favor of military deployment.

3 The Armed Wing
of the Informal Economy

Preamble

———

The Mexican state's estrangement from its police is expressed in public policies that, if they were the actions of an individual, would be attributed to a psychiatric illness: bipolar disorder, or clinical depression, apathy, and so forth. These policies oscillate between moments of feverish reform—expressed in constant shifts in strategy, new designs for police uniforms, spiraling investments in novel equipment, creation of specialized units—and periods of exasperation, discouragement, and passivity provoked by those reforms' paltry results.

In her study of policing, published in 2004, anthropologist Elena Azaola Garrido traced this back and forth movement for the case of Mexico City. So, for instance, when René Monterrubio was chief of the Metropolitan Police (1993–94), he created the Bengala and Transformación 2000 special-ops groups to prosecute car and bank robberies; the Bengala group was later disbanded because of its links to car theft. The next police chief, David Garay (1994–96), created the Grupo Pantano, which was disbanded in 1997 after being accused of involvement in several kidnappings. Police chief Rodolfo de Bernardi (1997–98) then created the Huracán, Mix, ORA, and Triángulo groups, which were all dissolved in 2001, and when it was Marcelo Ebrard's turn to lead the police (2002–4), he replaced Grupo Alfa with Grupos Operativos Especiales and Fuerzas Especiales, and created the Sagitario unit, the Policía Turística, and the Charra and Ribereña police forces. Grupos Operativos Especiales was disbanded in 2004, and replaced by the Unidad de Análisis Táctico. Grupo Tigre replaced Sagitario, and Grupo Marte and Grupo Sombra were newly created. Finally, when it was Joel Ortega's turn to head the force (2004–8), at the time of Azaola Garrido's study, he created the Citizen Protection Units and the Unit of Investigation against Kidnapping.[1] This mania for change and reform suggests an inability to stay the course with any consistent policy, and it reflects a cumulative history of failures that repeatedly plunged the government into despair and has consistently led it to favor militarization of policing as its best option.

Another effect of these dizzying stories of frustrated reforms is that the police have been left very vulnerable, as is manifested in the inordinately high number of police officers who are killed each year, as well as in the public indifference to the police force's plight. These figures are simply shocking. In 2020, there were 524 police officers killed; in 2019, 446; in 2018, 452; and in 2017, 530. The corresponding figures in the United States, which is a much more violent place than Europe or East Asia, are 45 in 2020, 51 in 2019, 53 in 2018, 45 in 2017, that is, about ten times fewer police officers killed in the United States than in

Mexico, and in a population that is roughly two and a half times larger than Mexico's.

Moreover, the types of violence that policemen face in Mexico are simply unparalleled in the United States, let alone in Europe or Asia. Police massacres have not been uncommon, nor have targeted attacks on local, state, and even federal police chiefs. Police chiefs have been murdered in Ensenada, Nogales, Culiacán, Mexico City, Ciudad Victoria, Torreón, Saltillo, and Chilpancingo, among other cities, as well as in many smaller municipalities, such as San Juan Evangelista (Veracruz), Quiroga (Michoacán), or Ciénega de Flores (Nuevo León), to name but a few in what is a surprisingly long list of cases. And then there are the modalities that such police killings take: there are police officers who have been strangled, kidnapped, tortured, disappeared, and dismembered. In some instances, policemen have been killed or tortured by members of other police forces or by the military. So, for example, in their study of seventy-seven cases of torture perpetuated by the armed forces, as documented by the National Human Rights Commission, sociologists Javier Treviño Rangel and Sara Velázquez Moreno note that eight of the torture victims—roughtly 10 percent—were police officers.[2]

The public's indifference to the massacre of policemen contrasts with the policemen's acute awareness of their own plight. Elena Azaola Garrido wrote that the Mexico City police that she interviewed had an oft-repeated saying: "The policeman has one foot in jail and the other in the graveyard."[3] The phrase is still used today, so much so that sociologist Corina Giacomello used it for the title of her book on Mexico's investigative police.[4] Tijuana policemen, for their part, instructed sociologist Oscar Contreras on the "three guarantees" that every policeman in that city has to know and understand: "They can kill you, fire you, or put you in jail at any time." Those are their three *guarantees*.[5] And in the face of all this, we have a society and a government that, if not entirely passive and indifferent, at the very least has minimized the magnitude and significance of these facts. The state's estrangement from its own police forces has had precisely this consequence.

In my remarks today I shall discuss the social dynamics that undergird the police's newfound precarious position. Specifically, I discuss how both the peaceful and the violent regulation of informal and illicit economies has changed and overwhelmed the police; I focus especially on the drug economy, which played a leading role in the transformation of the Mexican state.

The Armed Branch of the Informal Economy

The police have always played a special role in regulating informal economic activities, although they have generally preferred not to intervene when the balance of power is too heavily weighted against them. For example, police rarely intervene in the cases of electricity theft for home use in shantytowns and squatter settlements. But wherever the police force has felt powerful enough to intervene, it steps in to regulate informal activities, giving preference to some players and limiting the access of others, and so contributing to the regulation of street commerce, street prostitution, alcohol sales, or drug dealing.

In all of these cases, the law has been a useful point of reference in negotiations. Indeed, the law has served both as an incentive for parties to negotiate with the police and as a helpful baseline for reaching agreements, rather than as a standard or principle that needs to be strictly upheld.

In its relations with the informal and illicit economies, the role of the police was not so much to ensure compliance with the law as to serve as an agent helping to regulate informal activities by forging terms of agreement between the government and the economic actors whom the government needs to tolerate. The police thereby orchestrate a territorial order for informal economic activities. The extraction of resources from actors whose activity is outside the law, whether through bribes or extortion, sets up a pricing mechanism for the regulation of tolerance, separating those actors whose activity is tolerated from those who are to be persecuted.

As we saw in lecture 2, in addition to the use of the law as a bargaining tool, the police have always relied on the use of force to get certain people off of the streets. However, if a person involved in informal economic activities could not afford to pay the preventive police or refused to pay their required fees, he or she might then be handed over to the judicial arm—made up of investigative police, prosecutors, and judges—who could then arrest the wayward actor and continue extorting him or her, though now for much higher fees.

In this way, the police gave shape to an order in which they protected, first and foremost, the sectors of society in the formal economy whose taxes politically obliged the police to protect them. In addition, the police protected rent-paying actors in the informal and illicit economies. And finally, they "cleaned" or "cleared" spaces to protect the rent payers, or to comply with any politically motivated order from their bosses.

In this system (which began to break down in the 1980s) the government also used the police effectively as a spur to encourage the consolidation of "popular" (informal) union organizations—in other words, to create cadres of political representatives within the informal sector—and thereby ensure that these organizations had a well-defined leadership with whom the government might negotiate political support in exchange for tolerance. Thanks to the police threat that always hung over the informal economy, society as a whole was politically well organized. Popularly elected politicians had the support of organized popular sectors, which they received in exchange for keeping open channels of negotiation with the leaders of the informal sector, who in turn were responsible for "disciplining their people." The police helped shape the contours of these popular organizations because independent street vendors preferred to join organizations that guaranteed them police toleration, even if they had to pay fees in exchange for membership.

Having said this, it is also true that the police have never been the only relevant law enforcement agent: there have always been actors in the formal and informal economies who hire private protection. The number and size of these private forces have skyrocketed alongside state estrangement from the police. According to the Instituto Nacional de Estadística y Geografía (INEGI), in 2016 there were 4,102 private security companies registered in Mexico, and they have continued to grow so much that by 2018 private security officers outnumbered municipal, state, and federal police.[6] The nature of these private organizations is not well-known, and we do not know how many are urban private security groups, how many are paramilitary organizations used to protect mining companies or landowners, or how many are mere fronts for organizations that are dedicated to the illicit economy. In addition to the business of private security, informal economy actors also depend on their own organizational capacities for protection. So, for example, the reason why the police are slow to crack down on illegal electricity tapping in poor neighborhoods is that the residents tend to protect that resource collectively. A police officer seeking to extort money from one household that illegally taps its electricity will most likely have to confront the whole block. Street vendors, for their part, often have their own enforcers, while prostitutes rarely operate alone, and their pimps protect their work-spaces. I will refer collectively to such variegated violent enforcers as constituting the "armed wing of the informal economy."

The Problem

There is still no comparative study of the various armed wings of the informal economy. We do not have an overview of which areas of economic activity rely on professional or semiprofessional vigilantes, or which ones self-organize defenses, have informal hired violence specialists, or get protection from neighborhood gangs. This is an issue that deserves attention, because in the new Mexican state these kinds of organized or semiorganized violence have become more prominent than they were previously.

There is ethnographic and historical evidence that the armed wings of the (organized) informal economy usually had well-established connections with the police: gangs of car thieves paid the police to allow them to work; private security in bars and brothels had their own agreements with the police; groups of thugs, or *porros*, in high schools and universities had close connections with the Federal Judicial Police and the Secret Service; thugs in trade unions or street vendors' groups likewise had their contacts with the police, either directly or through their organizations' leaders.

The fluidity of the relationship between informal thugs and the police is on display in Mexico's newspaper crime pages, the *nota roja*; however, from the 1990s onward, a new situation emerged in which entire police departments were either neutralized or taken over outright by armed wings of the informal economy and specifically by what is known as "organized crime" or "narcos." I now turn to explore how this change came about.

Territorial Control Is Control Over the Police

For decades, the relationship between the armed wings of informal organizations and the police was, if not stable, at least routinized. That changed between the 1980s and 1990s. In part, this was a result of neoliberal reform, a process that, by 1994, would lead to a democratic transition that generated more competition between political parties and, consequently, greater contestation for political support from the informal economy's various organizations. As this rivalry increased, sectors of the organized informal economy were encouraged to promote their own candidates for electoral office. So, for example, anthropologist Salvador Maldonado writes that in Michoacán, which was one of the first states in which the Partido de la Revolución Democrática (PRD) unseated the Partido Revolucionario Institucional (PRI), during the 1990s it was already common to hear that the "cartels" paid money to political parties in exchange for their adopting slates that included their candidates for municipal governments and union leadership positions.[7]

An increasing number of municipalities came to be governed by the candidates of organized crime, which also meant that their police forces were appointed by them. In such cases, the municipal police could no longer play their old role of mediating between market pressure, political loyalty, and the law, as they had done earlier, but instead consistently bowed to the orders of their new bosses. They were now beholden to the interest of a very specific sector of the economy.

A recent study of insecurity in the city of Culiacán offers a glimpse of what is at stake in this shift in police alliances. Sociologists Iliana Padilla and Nelson Arteaga studied two contrasting areas of that city: the Zona Sur (Southern Zone), which is poorer, has a lot of small and informal commerce, and a high proportion of residents with criminal records; and the Sector Centro (Central Sector), which has upscale shops and restaurants and is a gathering point for wealthy people, including the so-called narco-juniors.[8] The Southern Zone is controlled by "los que andan mal" (those who have taken a wrong turn), an expression that can be interpreted either to suggest that the area is controlled by a large criminal organization—for example, the so-called Sinaloa Cartel—or else that it is controlled by any one specific boss—"la gente de fulano" (so-and-so's people). The Central Sector, on the other hand, is not a territory that is governed by *los que andan mal*, and the state and municipal police remain in charge of its security.

The implications of this difference are quite interesting. The merchants of the Southern Zone—the narco-controlled zone—feel more secure than those in the Central Sector, because in the Southern Zone the traders pay rent to organized crime. And since organized crime rules over the police, the police in that area have become allies of the small merchants and support them in their fight against petty crime. In other words, in the Southern Zone, organized crime has taken over the police and, in exchange for a rent, has aligned the police with the local merchants. This alliance reduces insecurity for these traders, who now have allies who have no qualms about killing petty thieves in order to cement their reputation as being effective security providers.

In the city's downtown, by contrast, local merchants feel insecure because they have to not only face petty crime but also negotiate with the police, who ask them for bribes and who, if they do not receive them, may also rob them. In addition, shopkeepers in the Central Sector may be put at risk by the son, wife, protégé, or lover of the big drug lords if they feel that they are not being properly looked after. In such an uncertain context, the control of a territory by organized crime can provide greater certainty than control by the police. On the other hand, territories controlled by organized crime like Culiacán's Southern Sector are spaces where there is no third party, no government arbiter, to which local merchants can appeal, so that a conflict with the de facto authorities is always a risk to avoid.

Two Functions of Drugs in the Transition to the New Regime

It can be said, without exaggeration, that drug trafficking was to the birth of Mexico's new regime what gold and silver from Mexico and Peru were to the rise of capitalism: like gold, drugs appeared as a fortuitous, external, factor that prompted an "original accumulation" of capital and power for the new regime.

Lately newspapers have finally begun to recognize that the term *narco-trafficking* does not adequately describe the activities of organized crime in Mexico, and that in reality it is engaged in a wide variety of businesses, from logging to mining to fishing, and from commercial agriculture to human trafficking. It is nonetheless true that drug trafficking played a unique role in the transition to the (in)security system that prevails today. This is due to the huge infusion of illegal money that entered the country through drug trafficking, particularly in the years of neoliberal transition (1980s–1990s), when the introduction of cocaine into Mexican trafficking (mid-1980s) coincided with a crisis in the Mexican countryside, a fact that made drug traffickers an irresistible financial resource for both peasants and ranchers.

So, for instance, in his description of the system of accumulation facilitated by the introduction of cocaine trafficking to

Michoacán, Romain Lecour Grandmaison calls drugs a "providential resource," applying a concept proposed by anthropologist Christian Geffray wherein a new resource generates such extreme social asymmetry that reciprocity ceases to be possible, because the new resource of exogenous origin is of incommensurable value with regard to those that circulated before.[9] This is what happened in the relationship between drug producers and traffickers and their neighbors, particularly once the drug trade added cocaine to the traditional marijuana economy, in the mid- to late 1980s. There was no way to compete with or repay the gifts offered by the narcos in those years of deep economic crisis and recession. The sudden influx of wealth also coincided with the beginnings of political liberalization and, later, the transition to democracy. This was also a factor in the qualitative leap in political power of the drug bosses, who transitioned from being beholden to local politicians to becoming their bosses, particularly in municipal governments.

And once a cacique or a grouping of narcos captured a local police force, it could easily begin to diversify its economic activities, so that drug trafficking networks moved into the business of selling protection, the theft of public resources, resource extractivism in violation of environmental norms, appropriation of public and private property, and the violent regulation of some markets—as well as into kidnapping, selling violent services to third parties, and the collection of tolls for access to roads, among other enterprises. Indeed, the drug economy fostered a form of business that relies on an, often temporary, territorial dominance that in turn relies crucially on the control of the local police and fosters businesses that are based on the capacity to create and dissipate insecurity. The ubiquitous term *narco* describes nothing more than the point of origin of a new way of regulating markets through the privatization or neutralization of the police.

Tarantella (The Dance of the Addicts)

In the 1980s and 1990s, there was still the idea in Mexico that drug addiction was a gringo thing. Mexicans might well be drunks, but they were not drug addicts. This prejudice was bolstered by a lack of knowledge of the physiological effects of the different drugs that were beginning to circulate and by a certain nationalistic hubris—and, of course, it turned out to be entirely false. Still, it is important to say something about why many Mexican drug traffickers today promote the sale of drugs in their own communities when they did not do so before.

Anthropologist Salvador Maldonado offers some relevant observations in his pioneering work on Michoacán, where the Knights Templar cartel imposed abstention as a requirement for joining their organization, even while they sold methamphetamines in the middle schools, and even in some grade schools, of the region.[10] Maldonado shows that the Knights Templar opened and closed meth drug sales to the *michoacano* youth and children according to their perception of whether or not the organization needed local support. When the Templars needed support, they shut down drug distribution in the schools.

In part, organized crime's interest in boosting domestic drug consumption obeyed a simple market logic: like any other producer, the drug trade faces crises of overproduction, which is why it is always in its interest to expand markets. But there is also another dimension to the issue, which has been less discussed. It is related not to the drug economy but to protection rackets.

The sale of protection is, as we have remarked, the touchstone of the new organized crime because protection is critical to both informal and illicit economies. This is the reason why control over local police is so important. But for protection to have value, there needs to be insecurity, and those who pay for protection need to feel that they cannot fend off dangers themselves. The sense of danger can be created directly by criminal organizations, of course, and it can also be generated by the police, as we have seen. However, if insecurity is caused solely by the police or by crime syndicates, society acquires a clearly defined enemy, and it may be tempted to organize emancipation movements, as happened in Michoacán in 2013 with the self-defense movements (the so-called *autodefensas*) that ended up overthrowing the Knights Templar organization. The monopoly of private protection is not easy to retain for extended periods, and constant reliance on brutality and terror can, under certain conditions, ignite a prarie fire of indignation.

For this reason, it is useful to have an independent source of *disorganized* insecurity. Drug addiction increases the incidence of petty crime and so acquires a double function. In addition to expanding the drug market, it consolidates the protection market. Drug retailing fosters disorganized crime, which then becomes a legitimizing force for organized crime. In the process, addiction swells the "criminal reserve army," that is, it creates a cheap source of casual labor for the drug cartels.

The shopkeepers of the Southern Zone of Culiacán—the one controlled by *los que andan mal* (the evildoers)—provided the sociologists who were studying them with a very clear analysis of this. These shopkeepers and peddlers distinguished between three kinds of criminals: the drug traffickers and their gunmen, to whom they paid rent; professional thieves (*rateros*); and the so-called *tarántulas*, who were drug addicts who stole opportunistically to feed their habit.[11] Before the Southern Zone was controlled by the narcos, local merchants were routinely burglarized by both professional thieves and *tarántulas*, as well as by the police. But once organized crime subdued the police, the criminals proceeded to kill "all the rats" (in other words, the professional thieves and the *tarántulas*), and there was relative safety for traders. That security translated, if not quite into legitimacy, at least into a good working relationship with organized crime.

In short, drugs played a key role in the transition to a new security economy, and they also played a critical role in the internal segmentation of the criminal world, in particular its division into three classes: one that we could call corporate and transnational ("organized crime"); one that we could call artisanal and local, composed of professional thieves (the *rateros*) and small neighborhood gangs; and one characterized by occasional and disorganized thievery, carried out by what in Culiacán they call *tarántulas*.

Back to the Police, but This Time the Judicial Police

We have seen that the so-called preventive police also have a criminal function. Corruption—which, being as it was systemic, was not strictly corruption—encouraged the preventive police to intervene in the event of any infringement of the law and then, instead of remitting the offender to the judiciary for punishment, take the law into their own hands and punish transgressors directly by extorting payments. In other words, the preventive police exceeded their normative functions, and served *not only to prevent or stop transgressions, but also to punish them.*

Given all of this, it is worth asking what the purpose of the ministerial or Judicial Police was, whose purported mission is to investigate crimes and catch criminals. If the preventive police regulated crime directly, through extortion, and if impunity rates for serious crimes in Mexico have been well above 90 percent for many decades now, then the answer to the question "What do the Judicial Police do?" is anything but obvious.[12]

Until the 2016 reforms, the Mexican criminal justice system was inquisitorial, meaning that public prosecutors (*fiscales* and *ministerios públicos,* or MPs) are the ones who can open criminal investigations. Against any suspect, they can order the investigative or Judicial Police and the various crime and lab experts whom they have at their disposal to carry out the inquiries that are required to resolve the case. Prosecutors may also call in witnesses to testify. Once an investigation file is complete, the MP sends it to a judge, who may ask for clarifications or again interrogate witnesses. The judge will then decide whether or not the accused is guilty and, if so, what his or her sentence will be. In other words, prison admissions necessarily go through the Judicial Police, since they are the ones who carry out the investigation for the public prosecutor's office, and they are also the ones who mediate between the orders of a prosecutor and the indicted suspects.

The Judicial Police are a much smaller presence than the preventive police, which at the end of the twentieth century made up 91 percent of all police forces.[13] They are also better paid and have higher educational requirements. In addition, the Judicial Police are allowed to wear plain clothes and use their badge (*charola*) for identification, a characteristic they have shared with some political or secret police forces, such as the now-defunct Dirección Federal de Seguridad (DFS).

Many elements of my earlier description of the preventive police apply to the Judicial Police—especially the characteristic hybridization between a modern bureaucratic organization and an ancien régime–style prebendal system, as well as between an economy characterized by the pricing of all bureaucratic transactions and a rhetoric that constantly frames police actions as personal favors. Those two characteristics are as relevant for the Judicial Police as they are for the preventive police, but I now seek an answer to a different question: Why did a differentiated protection business develop between the preventive and Judicial Police?

The answer to this question is related to three different factors: (1) the Judicial Police, formerly the Ministerial Police, is the only agency capable of taking an offender to jail; (2) thanks to its direct relationship with suspects who have been (or are about to be) indicted, the Judicial Police has close relations with politics and, indirectly, also with the media; and (3) the Judicial Police is under the direct command of the governors and the president of the republic, through state and federal attorneys general, and so is not subject to municipal control.

The system of regulation organized by the preventive police revolves around the exploitation of any transgression of law:

the preventive police negotiate payments in exchange for letting transgressions pass, so it can be said that the preventive police make a living out of *not* taking offenders to the public prosecutor's office, which is why they tend to avoid documentation of their actions as much as possible.

The Judicial Police, on the other hand, have a close relationship not only with the prison system but also with all the documents that go into an investigative file. The Judicial Police respond to requests from the public prosecutor's office, and then investigate—and/or extort money from—suspects. But in addition to mediating between prosecutors and criminals (by investigating, capturing, beating, or extorting the latter), the judicial policemen and policewomen work for long hours writing reports and delivering ordinances. According to the ethnography carried out by legal scholar Catalina Pérez Correa in two public prosecutors' offices in Mexico City, Judicial Police officers spend most of their time composing files, while their work investigating the crimes that the public calls in is often non-existent.[14] Impunity rates for serious crimes are currently calculated at 96 percent. For some crimes, conviction rates are practically nil. Up until and through the current year (2021), there have been only thirty-six convictions for the more than 93,000 disappearances that have accrued so far. At other times, the Judicial Police's role is to report to the crime scene as soon as possible, in order to receive money from either victims or perpetrators in exchange for writing up a report that suits the interests of the highest bidder.

Let us now turn to take a look at what this all means for the role of the judiciary in regulating the drug economy. Historian

Benjamin Smith has proposed a chronology for the development of Mexico's drug protection rackets that begins with an era when local political bosses (caciques), who controlled the municipal presidencies of their localities, used that power to appoint their own enforcers (*pistoleros*) to the municipal police, as well as to negotiate with state politicians, and so make space for drug production and smuggling.[15]

However, as the volume of drug production increased and the profits from the business grew, the business attracted the attention of the governors, particularly in the main marijuana- and poppy-producing states, as well as in the border states through which those products would have to pass in order to reach their market. According to Smith's account, those governors ended up taking over the protection business, wresting it from local caciques. This process of appropriation would also trigger the entry of the (state) Judicial Police into the business of regulating drug trafficking, since the Judicial Police force could operate as the enforcement arm of the state government because it is beyond municipal control.

The third moment in Smith's periodization is the transition from control of drug production and transportation by state governments to federal control, now exercised by the federal police and the armed forces. For most of the twentieth century, there was little presence of the Policía Judicial Federal, or Federal Judicial Police, throughout the Mexican territory, because there were few crimes that were defined as federal crimes. The federal police's main tasks were performed by the customs police, the federal highway police, and the banking police. And federal efforts to prosecute drug trafficking, developed in response to US pressure from the 1940s onward, relied on the military, rather than on the Federal Judicial Police.

That situation began to change from the 1970s onward, due —following Smith's thesis—to the increase in the size of the drug business, which attracted increasingly weightier politicians. There was also, it seems to me, a second factor, which was the diversification of trafficking routes and the territorial expansion of crops and labs. The result was that the Federal Judicial Police grew and began to concentrate mainly on regulating drug trafficking. For its part, the DFS, which was supposed to be an intelligence agency, also grew enormously and devoted itself to the investigation of other federal crimes, such as human trafficking, car theft, and smuggling.[16] However, as these crimes were often linked to one another—the same criminal organization specialized in drug trafficking, human trafficking, and car theft, for instance—there was a lot of porosity and exchange between these two federal agencies.

The last phase in Smith's interpretation begins in 1985, after the assassination of DEA intelligence agent Kiki Camarena by a drug cartel and the dissolution of the DFS by President Miguel de la Madrid, in response to its corruption. The president's action gave rise to violent competition for protection between the various state, local, and federal police forces, as well as the armed forces (army and navy), weakening the effectiveness of all of these entities. This process in turn led to the dispersion of criminal organizations throughout the national territory, as well as to the capture of pieces of the state by organized crime, especially municipal governments and some sectors of state and federal government administrations.

This is not the place to evaluate Smith's interpretation—his book is a landmark in the historiography of drug trafficking in Mexico. I seek only to use some of his findings to help us understand why the Judicial Police and, at a certain point, the secret police (DFS) played different roles than the municipal and preventive police in regulating the drug economy.

We begin with the first transition described by Smith, from local protection for drug production—at the hands of the local cacique or municipal president—to protection from the state government. The protector-cacique was usually also a drug producer: he grew marijuana or poppy, and was well connected to the other producers in his municipality. This kind of cacique also had some influence over transportation in his municipality: he had access to local airstrips where planes might land and kept tabs on the local truckers, bus and taxi drivers, and owners of petrol stations, and so he could help or hinder local producers in their business, leaning particularly on his control of the municipal police.

In this sense, the local cacique was only primus inter pares, or first among equals, as anthropologist Paul Friedrich suggested half a century ago in his classic ethnography of an agrarian community in Michoacán.[17] The cacique was not a unique or singular personage but rather a dominant figure from among a group or class of local "princes" (to use Friedrich's Machiavelli-inspired language), who were intertwined by relations of friendship, kinship, or rivalry. Caciques in drug-producing regions were thus not solitary characters but leaders of a social class.

Moreover, all of them operated in regions where agrarian reform had been implemented (a process that in Mexico peaked in the 1930s), so that land concentration was legally limited and politically regulated. Moreover, marijuana and poppy crops tended to be dispersed in the sierras, especially in the western Sierra Madre. This fragmentation of both crops and agrarian property reinforced plurality rather than hyperconcentration within the cacique class, a fact that is clearly portrayed in Adele Blázquez's ethnography of Badiraguato, Sinaloa, where each ranch has its *pesado* ("man of weight," or here we could say "member of a cacique class"), who is usually also the owner of the local convenience store, the loan shark who advances money to poppy-growing peasants, the buyer of their opium gum, and the protector—with his gunmen—of the ranch where both the *pesado* himself and the peasant families live. The strength of the cacique who achieved control over the municipal presidency is manifested in his ability to marginalize some *pesados* and ally himself with others, as well as in his relationships with politicians in the state capital. If the armed strength of his various allied or dependent gunmen was not enough to build a winning alliance, he would either have to succumb to the bullets of a rival or support an alternative leader.

Once the drugs were shipped out of the producers' municipality, however, the smugglers who transported them depended on other social networks, and especially on their contacts on or near the US-Mexico border. These networks fostered or relied on a second protection business that was structured according to the specific requirements of border trafficking. These two logics—control of the productive area and protected access to international smuggling—together constituted, broadly speaking, the protection system in the early era of the drug trade.

As a result, any governor who wished to retain some degree of control over drug trafficking needed to reorganize the protection business so that he might articulate production to international trafficking. He could do this either by controlling all of the main drug trafficking routes out of his state, or by punishing producers and traffickers who did not want to pay him rent and then using them to show the federal or US authorities that drug trafficking was being duly prosecuted in his state.

Either way, the governor had to rely on the Judicial Police, who reported directly to his attorney general and so were beyond the control of local caciques. The state's prisons were also at the disposal of the state attorney general, and they too became an important resource in the complicated interplay between a regulated tolerance of the drug market and the repression required to calm the political pressure against trafficking coming from the United States and from its interlocutors in Mexico's federal government.

However, no one governor's attempt to control the drug market in his state was ever successfully achieved because—unlike the local caciques, who were members of a social class that had territorial, commercial, and political control in their producing areas—the Judicial Police were not firmly rooted locally, and they had to be intimidating enough to force deals with a whole class of local caciques and smugglers.

Unlike the preventive police, the Judicial Police could not keep up a constant physical presence except on a few roads and at customs offices. They were insufficient in number for the functions they now had to perform, a fact that opens a vista onto a process that is fundamental to the story that I am telling here, but that has not yet been sufficiently researched. The key to that story is the rise of the figure of the so-called *madrina* (godmother). The term refers to the practice of distributing police badges to individuals who were neither policemen nor government employees, but who were informally (and illegally) subcontracted in order to assist the Judicial Police in their tasks, in exchange for a piece of their business. Due to its newfound role in the drug economy, the Judicial Police had to extend its use of informally hired helpers, or *madrinas*, and that involved not merely giving them badges but allowing them to share police identity and police prerogatives.

The growth in numbers of these "godmothers" is an example of a specific modality of the outsourcing of violence to specialists. The informal labor market for violence grew in tandem with the illicit economy, which was beginning to be regulated by the Judicial Police either in alliance or in competition with the old caciques. In response to the growing need for enforcers, the Judicial Police developed its own informal armed wing, composed of *madrinas*, which was controlled in a decentralized manner by police commanders. This development allowed the Judicial Police to become flexible enough to try to regulate the drug economy in some states and to embark on various, often illegal, operations when and where they were required. There was, however, a price to be paid for this arrangement, which was less central control over the police due to the proliferation of a decentralized network of godmothers. There was, too, an inevitable rise in the use of excessive police force directed against anyone singled out by the state attorney general, but also against any personal rival of a policeman or godmother. The Judicial Police thus inspired a nebulous but widespread sense of dread, since it was a force at once centrally directed and feral, undirected. Both protected and licentious.

The rise of the so-called godmothers is a key development, the history of which has not yet been investigated. The phenomenon marks the beginning of the process of privatization of a number of public goods, starting with public security itself, and the *madrinas'* example would eventually be incorporated into the business model of that constellation of criminal organizations known today as cartels. As a hypothesis, I suggest that this process began with the multiplication of godmothers in the Judicial Police, a development that responded to the need to regulate the buoyant drug trade of the 1970s and 1980s. Up until that point the existing Judicial Police forces were too small and insufficient for such a task. Moreover, having their own informally hired armed wing gave the Judicial Police greater freedom, especially when it came to killing or torturing, or to carrying out sudden, unexpected raids. The *madrinas* were a kind of budding modality of paramilitarism.

The story of the informalization of the Judicial Police began with the *madrinas*, but then moved on to the distribution of badges not only to the godmothers who joined the Judicial Police's operations but also to police allies within the drug trade itself. We know of several examples of this. For instance, when the army raided El Búfalo ranch in Chihuahua, owned by the notorious drug trafficker Rafael Caro Quintero, they found a number of armed guards who carried badges from the DFS, whose job was to patrol El Búfalo's several thousand enslaved laborers.[18]

In his book on the DFS, Sergio Aguayo tells how, when that agency was dissolved in 1985, a highly sensitive operation was set up to "collect the *charolas*" (badges) from a number of high-ranking individuals who were not at all involved in police operations. Among them were politicians, journalists, and artists. Many badges were also distributed among the drug lords who were allied to the secret police.[19] Once all these badges were collected, alongside those of the *madrinas* of the DFS, Pedro Vázquez Colmenares, the first head of DISEN (Dirección de Investigación y Seguridad Nacional), the new organization created to substitute for the DFS, "decided that the old badges of the DFS agents and surrogates would be melted down and used to make a statue of Juárez."[20]

The gesture of pouring the brass from the badges into a mold of President Benito Juárez is a paradigmatic example of the voluntarist reading of police reform that then prevailed and still carries the day in Mexico, a reading that imagines that the deformities of institutions like the DFS or the Judicial Police are due to the corruption of their personnel, and that it is enough to put the police under an honest leadership to melt the corruption and mold the raw material of which it was made—the policeman—into a heroic republican agent, capable of guaranteeing the rule of law (embodied, paradigmatically, in the person of the citizen-president Benito Juárez). But the deformities of the DFS and the Judicial Police ultimately stemmed from their role as regulatory agencies of an enormous illicit economy. The problem, in other words, was not individual dishonesty, but the institution's regulatory function.

Even so, it is nonetheless true that police leadership matters, although not always with the expected results, as the desire for honesty has often led to the sacking of especially violent or corrupt Judicial Police officers and godmothers. These dismissals have in turn fed the informal market of violence specialists. It did not take long for fired DFS *madrinas* and Judicial Police officers to find other jobs, either in the thriving business of private security companies or in organized crime. Indeed, it is no coincidence that the first 1980s crime wave in Mexico City happened just as the famous DFS was disbanded. The brand-new bronze statue of Benito Juárez that symbolically inaugurated the federal government's newfound commitment to the rule of law also launched a new way of organizing the drug economy, which passed into the hands of a new type of criminal organization.

Three Theses

First Thesis

I am finally ready to offer a summary statement of the ideas presented so far. My first thesis has been that the drug economy was the branch of the illicit economy that finally destabilized the old policing system that had prevailed in Mexico for most of the twentieth century. There were two characteristics of the drug economy that allowed it to play this role: on the one hand, its size, flexibility, and elasticity, and on the other, its transnational and international complexity.

Each of these dimensions had destabilizing effects on the police. The first—the size and growth potential of the drug economy—led the Judicial Police to develop its own informal sector, made up not only of paid informants and allies in the criminal world but also of an informal modality of paramilitarization by way of the so-called godmothers, or *madrinas*.

This characteristic of the Mexican Federal Judicial Police—its intimate cohabitation with informality—requires an articulation between a legal, official, bureaucratic core ("the corporation") and a constellation of informally subcontracted dependents, coordinated with greater or lesser efficiency by individual police commanders. In this respect, the Mexican police was like many other Mexican institutions that depend on informal workers for practically everything.

My hypothesis is that the informal reserve army of the police—the lumpen police force that was made up of the so-called *madrinas*—grew hand in hand with the drug trafficking economy. Increased reliance on informal subcontracting also diminished central control over policing, leading to more and more rogue police operatives until, due to a series of political pressures, the informally contracted police were either severed from or bid out of the police forces to which they had been appended and then moved into the violent and specialized labor pool that could be hired by what we call organized crime.

The collapse of police control over public safety (such as it was) began at the moment when the relationship between the formal police apparatus ("the corporation") and its informal reserve army ("the lumpen police") broke down. This fracture was caused at once by the reorientation of organized crime toward a transnational economy and by the increasingly vocal social pressure for governments to professionalize the police, generally without having sufficiently considered the delicate situation in which the police corporations would find themselves if they were forced to divest from their informal reserve army and hand it over to private entrepreneurs instead.

Second Thesis
The drug economy has the particularity of being a key factor in Mexico's bilateral relationship with the United States, a country that, from the early 1940s, placed illegal drugs at the heart of its international agenda. Unlike movement of other types of contraband, drug trafficking strikes a particularly sensitive nerve in a bilateral relationship that is indispensable for the survival of any Mexican government.

Until a couple of decades ago, drug production in Mexico was almost exclusively oriented toward the US market. As a result, it was an activity that was economically beneficial from the Mexican point of view, so that the pressure to eradicate it basically came from abroad. Drug consumption was understood to be an "American thing," whose negative consequences could be kept at a distance from Mexican society. Thus, governors, such as Sinaloa's Leopoldo Sánchez Celis (in office from 1963 to 1968), promoted strong antivice campaigns in their home states, while taking a lead role in the drug trade.[21] Sinaloa was at that time the epicenter of heroin and marijuana production in Mexico, but it was also a state where bars and brothels were shut down to maintain a "healthy local environment." Drugs did not, then, have a negative effect on local society. And, despite the rise of drug addiction inside Mexico, the combination of intense external political pressure and local economic benefit still sets the drug economy off from almost any other branch of the informal economy.

Since political pressure against Mexico's drug economy coursed primarily through diplomatic channels, this pressure was felt first and foremost in the upper echelons of the federal government, in Mexico City, and was then filtered indirectly onto local politics. The police force that was in charge of regulating trafficking thus had to be capable of responding to contradictory demands: political pressure from the federal government and economic opportunities provided by drug trafficking.

This mediating function between diplomatic pressure and economic interests was the reason why the Judicial Police were able to acquire a dominant role in regulating the drug economy vis-à-vis the local caciques: they were ultimately under the command of the governors or the federal executive and could therefore serve as buffers between the pressure and opportunities stemming from the local order and the international agenda brought to bear on the president of the republic. Mediation between these two forces gave the police access to a lot of cash and also to drugs that they could either sell or consume, but it also placed them in a complicated situation vis-à-vis government officials who had to respond more directly to diplomatic pressures coming from the United States.

The police could either help assuage this pressure by joining in the antidrug crusade or ignore US-backed federal directives, so as to operate as semiautonomous agents. My second thesis is that, in response to the pressures for reform that the police began to face during the governments of Miguel de la Madrid (1982–88), Carlos Salinas de Gortari (1988–94), and Ernesto Zedillo (1994–2000), many key police operators moved from selective compliance to quiet subversion.

Third Thesis

In its early years, Mexican drug traffic was ultimately controlled by groups of smugglers belonging to ethnic enclaves that were well established in the United States: Chinese "mafias" with experience in the opium trade, as well as Italian, Russian, Jewish, and other mafias. These traffickers allied themselves with Mexican producers while they remained in charge of distributing certain drugs in the United States.

After that early moment, trafficking passed into Mexican hands, thanks to the consolidation of transnational migratory circuits and the intensification of trade between Mexico and the United States. Mexican producers of heroin or marijuana could smuggle their product into the United States using either migrants from their hometown as "mules" or resorting to networks of professional smugglers who had been operating for years in all the cities along the border. The existence of Mexican communities in the West and Southwest United States helped drug trafficking networks capture some of the profits from wholesale sales in the United States.

From the mid-1980s onward, Colombian mafias turned to Mexico as a favored route to smuggle their cocaine into the United States, but that decision required building alliances in Mexico. Cocaine was the first drug trafficked by Mexicans that was not locally produced. As a result, Mexican drug trafficking networks now opened up to the south—to Colombia and Central America—and then, with the trafficking of precursor chemicals for methamphetamines and fentanyl, to China. The globalization of the drug economy—a process that has continued to diversify—facilitated traffic in expertise, at first from Colombia to Mexico, involving even the importation of a Colombian nomenclature now commonly used in Mexico, with terms such as *cartel* and *sicario*. That then progressed to the importation of specialists; for instance, there was the recruitment of elite Guatemalan army troops—the infamous Kaibiles—or, more recently, Colombian gangs who specialize in the extortion of small informal businesses through the management of microcredits. Today, Mexican organizations have commercial relations and investments on five continents, with a particularly strong presence in several Central and South American countries, and Mexican drug traffickers have become the main suppliers of drugs throughout the United States.

My third and final thesis is that the transnationalization of the drug economy made it impossible for either state police or federal Judicial Police to control the business effectively and led to the growing complexity of criminal networks and organizations. It is true that the new complexity of criminal organizations remains mysterious—the ubiquity of the term *cartel* elides much more than it reveals. However, the deconstructive counterposition, which insists that the term *cartel* is little more than a DEA invention, created for political purposes, and that there are no cartels but rather "a market for drugs and people who work in it," seems in the end not to be very illuminating.[22]

Looking at the issue more closely, it is clear that there has been not one but several trends of change within drug trafficking networks. One narrative, developed by Guadalupe Correa-Cabrera in her book on the Zetas, argues that, until that organization was founded (in the late 1990s), the dominant model of trafficking organizations was that of Sinaloa, which according to the author was a vertical organization, whose hierarchy was based on kinship and fictive kinship (*compadrazgo*) relationships and informal patron-client networks. The Zetas revolutionized this scheme, militarizing their command and operations and expanding their "business portfolio" from drug trafficking to the protection business and extortion in general and, from there, to the illegal exploitation of resources in forms as diverse as gasoline theft, illegal coal mining, human trafficking, and arms trafficking.[23]

I would add that the competition between these two organizational models led to the socialization of the innovations of each: militarization in the various Sinaloa organizations, with the recruitment of professionals not only from the Mexican army but also from Guatemala's Kaibiles and Colombia's Revolutionary Armed Forces (FARC), but also competition between Mexican cartels to link up with rival US-based gangs, such as the Mara Salvatrucha (MS-13), Barrio 18, the Mexicles, or Los Aztecas. Transnational criminal organizations have gained a level of flexibility, around both sites of production and routes of distribution, that they did not have in the early era, and this flexibility also limits the usefulness of state Judicial Police and puts a heavier burden on federal organizations—either federal police or the armed forces.

In addition, the wars between various criminal organizations, which were conditioned and sharpened by the Mexican government's so-called war on drugs, led to a process of fragmentation and territorial dispersion and to the creation of many local organizations that do not have the capacity to move products in the transnational arena. They are mainly dedicated to the extraction of local resources. The fact that we use the term *cartel* to refer to all of this organizational diversity, or refer to all of these groups together simply as "organized crime," confuses the analysis.

Finally, the extension of organized crime from drug trafficking into the protection business necessarily implies the neutralization or outright capture of municipal police forces, and this in turn has opened the door to intense conflicts between municipal and state police, a fact that became a stimulus for organizations to seek to control entire state governments. These two developments, the practice of capturing municipal police and the conflicts between state and municipal police, have opened a new page in our history, which is the great massacre of policemen occurring year after year—a phenomenon that is as much a core characteristic of our violence as is the murder of journalists, political candidates, and grassroots environmental defenders.

4 Regional Systems of the Criminal Economy

n 1964–65 anthropologist G. William Skinner published three articles on the relationship between marketing systems and social structure in rural China, in which he proved conclusively that "the village" was not an adequate unit of analysis for economic, political, or cultural study.[1] Instead, Skinner discovered that, in agrarian China, social reproduction developed in a space that he called "a standard marketing region," which was a heterogeneous space composed of a number of peasant villages, articulated economically, politically, and socially by a central market that was usually situated in a small city. As a result, the village—which up until then had been the primary locus of anthropological analysis of "traditional Chinese culture"—turned out to be but a fragment of a larger structure, and village culture was just one manifestation of a provincial culture that generally had its epicenter in a small city.

Taking my inspiration from this vintage discovery, I shall argue that analyses of Mexican violence and criminality have incurred an error similar to the one that Skinner identified all those years ago: they concentrate their attention on a unit of analysis that is incomplete and is but a fragment of a broader structure. Our students of criminality tend to start from a typology of crime organizations in order to concentrate their attention on one specific type or another: transnational crime organizations, for instance, or neighborhood gangs.

Too often, their next step is the reification of these categories, so that the differences between organizations of a single "type" are prone to get blurred to such a degree that, today, we use the term *cartel* to identify groups that are dedicated to stealing gasoline (the Cartel of Santa Rosa de Lima, for instance), groups that organize the international commerce of cocaine (the Cartel del Golfo of the 1990s, for example), or groups that combine human trafficking, gasoline theft, protection rackets, and drug trafficking, such as the Zetas or the Cartel Jalisco Nueva Generación. The mystification of the term *cartel* has succeeded to such an extent that today any criminal group that wants to ratchet up its prestige has but to carry out a few deeds of scandalous violence to graduate to being thought of as "a cartel." The term *gang* has an equally ample set of referents. The result is that it is hard to come up with an analytically useful definition of what constitutes a cartel, a gang, or even what the connection is between petty crime and organized crime.

Recognizing this difficulty, some scholars have worked to deconstruct the typologies that have been put forth by criminologists and in the media, showing that reified terms such as *cartel* and *gang* are often deployed for ideological or propagandistic purposes. However, deconstructive efforts tend to retain or accept diffuse and imprecise views of the social organizational forms that have been invented in order to regulate illicit economies.[2] Sometimes we get the impression that the self-described "critical scholarship" adheres to the tenet that only state institutions are capable of coordinating or inventing new forms of criminal organization, that the state is the fons et origo (source and origin) of any and all of them, so that only state organizations deserve to be described, analyzed, and subjected to critical scrutiny.

In today's lecture I distance myself both from the dominant —let's call it the reified—position regarding the cartels and the deconstructivist critique of that position, in order to put forward some elements for a regional analysis of criminal economies. Specifically, I shall identify four types of contrasting "criminal subregions" that are the principal spaces of articulation of the illicit transnational economy that now has Mexico as a hub.

Units of Analysis of Organized and Disorganized Crime

In my previous lecture I proposed a rough typology of the field of organized crime. It is composed, first, of a sophisticated type of organization, transnationally integrated and with an international scope, that I characterized as "corporate" or even "industrial." I then identified a second kind of crime organization that is rooted locally or within a confined region, in the mode of either gangs or professional rustlers or thieves, and that I characterized as "artisanal." Finally, there is an atomized and not professionalized set of actors devoted to opportunistic thefts, frequently impelled by drug addiction, that I referred to either as a "lumpen criminal" class or as a "criminal reserve army." I shall now turn to a few contrasting ways in which these three sorts of organizations are combined. I do so with the aim of understanding the spatial dimension of the social organization forms that create, shape, and develop illicit economies.

Historic Arc

Our object of study is the ways in which criminal economies are spatially structured. To focus on this objective, I consider four interconnected regional subsystems. Before setting out to do this, however, it is useful to recall that regional systems are by their very nature changing processes, and for this reason it is important to specify their historical parameters—in this case, the parameters that are relevant to Mexico's criminal regional systems, in particular. Once we have covered this ground, we can move on to the specifics of our typology.

During its first era, which spanned most of the twentieth century, Mexican drug trafficking had two components, one agricultural and the other commercial, oriented to taking marijuana and heroin, which were the two drugs that Mexico produced, across the US border. The second era began in the mid-1980s, and it added to the marijuana/heroin repertoire the trafficking of an imported drug, whose raw material cannot be grown in Mexico: cocaine. This new product required an expansion and sophistication of commercial and smuggling activities, and it also transformed the geography of Mexico's drug economy that had, until the 1980s, been disproportionately controlled by Sinaloa-centered drug producers, moving up and down northwestern and north-central Mexico. The rise of the cocaine trade provided opportunities for illegal networks that were centered in Mexico's northeastern state of Tamaulipas, because their smugglers could now bring a product from Colombia and smuggle it into the United States without having to purchase either marijuana or heroin from the producers who controlled it in the western Sierra Madre, that is, in Sinaloa, Chihuahua, and Durango. This second era also involved extending the networks of Mexico's smugglers, both within the United States and southward, through Central America into Colombia or points even farther south. Mexican smugglers so succeeded in broadening their networks that they are today the main providers of illegal drugs throughout the United States, and not just in the Southwest, as was formerly the case.[3]

This second era is also important because of the invention of crack cocaine that was cheap enough to allow for the development of a plebeian market for hard drugs within Mexico itself. The opening of this internal market provided an outlet for merchandise when there was overproduction. Moreover, the exponential growth of the value of the drug economy in the 1980s made marijuana and cocaine into a kind of currency that could be used by crime networks to pay off associates, including police and politicians. These allies in turn would only accept such payments if they could unload the drugs onto local markets.

Finally, the development of an internal market within Mexico also became an instrument of legitimation for organized crime, because drug addicts began to swell the ranks of small-time thieves, since they sometimes needed to steal in order to feed their habit, and so they became a justification for organized crime's movement into the protection racket.

Indeed, this lumpen criminal stratum of drug addicts has a double role: it serves as a criminal reserve army, used equally as hired hands by criminal organizations and police, and it allows the police to fill jails with inmates that can serve long sentences whenever the judicial apparatus needs to show that it is "doing something" against crime. In 2016, Mexico's bureau of statistics (INEGI) carried out a survey among the inmates of Mexico's brimming prisons, and 52 percent said that they had been jailed on false charges, while a full 44 percent of the 210,000 inmates who are withering in Mexico's jails—often not without first having been tortured by the police—were consigned for *narcomenudeo* (selling drugs on the street), a term that is deployed by the police as if it were a synonym of drug addict.[4]

In short, cocaine trafficking was an innovation that affected more than just the scope and reach of Mexican drug trafficking: it also sparked a deep change in the socio-spatial organization of criminality, with the formation of an entire stratum of scapegoats that can, additionally, easily be recruited by organized crime. In other words, the introduction of cocaine led to the consolidation of a criminal reserve army. The members of this new class of the "lumpen-criminalizable" are today the most common kind of sacrificial offering that is presented by politicians and the police to society, in order to satisfy its insatiable thirst for punitive measures on the altar of Order. "Punitive populism," a political impulse that today encompasses the entire spectrum of Mexico's political parties, has political rivals striving to fill prisons in order to win elections or distract public opinion. For a mafioso, a policeman, or a politician, sacrificing an addict is easily done, and the ritual of imprisoning them, or even of slaughtering them, has become a standard recourse to quell social criticism.

The third and current era in our broad history of drug trafficking begins with Mexico's entry into the methamphetamine and fentanyl business. That innovation was made possible by an organizational form that had existed since Mexico's entry to the cocaine trade, the so-called cartel. Now commercial networks extended to China, in a trade relationship that also opened up a new export market for illegally extracted raw materials such as lumber or iron ore, while developing new productive spaces in Mexico, such as the labs, where the precursor drugs are processed.

The first era of our historical arc, which lasted from the early twentieth century to around 1985, was characterized by the articulation of an agro-productive—marijuana and poppy growing—sector and a commercial sector specialized in contraband that moved the merchandise from productive regions in the western Sierra Madre to the US-Mexico border.

The second era gave more power to smuggling, given the complexities of having to move cocaine from Colombia to Mexico and from its various points of arrival in Mexico into the United States. It was during this second era that Mexico's richest drug-running organizations began to be called cartels, in imitation of their Colombian counterparts. These organizations also began to serve as wholesalers for drugs that would be distributed and consumed within Mexico itself.

During the third moment in our historical arc, the prominence of smuggling and selling remained, except that the business was now tied to Chinese producers, in addition to the Colombians. The development of an internal market continued apace, now oriented principally toward the consumption of methamphetamines, a market that grew 775 percent from 2000 to 2021, and has even overtaken local consumption of marijuana.[5] In this third moment, organized crime also opened new extractivist lines of business—illegal mining, fishing, logging, and so on—wherein its armed power is used to break environmental laws and to appropriate protected public goods in order either to sell them in local markets or to export them to China. Also, a new productive space developed in the form of meth labs, some of which have been set up in old agro-productive regions that were already controlled by the drug organizations.

This third era also magnified the importance of Mexico's Pacific ports. Indeed, while the second—cocaine-dominated—era contributed to "heat up" Mexico's southern borders, along with a number of ports and fishing villages in the Caribbean and Gulf coasts, the third, methamphetamine, era heated up the Pacific ports that do trade with China, such as Salina Cruz, Lázaro Cárdenas, Colima, and Mazatlan, and it has made Mexico's Pacific the country's third "hot border." In the first era of drug trafficking, only the US-Mexico border mattered; the second era brought intense traffic to Mexico's southern border and its ports and fishing villages on the Gulf Coast; the third era brought on a protracted conflict for control over the major shipping ports on the Pacific Coast.

The regional analysis of criminal organizations that I shall now propose relies on understanding this broad arc, composed of three great moments in Mexican drug trafficking, because, as we saw in lecture 3, drug trafficking was the activity that transformed the shape and scale of Mexico's crime organizations and that gave birth to its new state form.

Four Subsystems of the Criminal Economy

1. The Subsystem with a Core in Retail
(Prototype: Los Angeles, California)

In order correctly to identify units of analysis—and move from the study of gangs or cartels to the study of their modes of integration—it is important to break the bad habit of setting the national territory as a limit to our thinking. This custom is ingrained in Mexican social sciences, and it is to offset this trend that I start this regional analysis outside of Mexico, in California, which was the core market for Mexican drugs until Mexico's drug organizations managed to marginalize their competitors across the entire United States.

The distribution of Mexican drugs in the United States always relied upon both wholesalers and retailers. Early on, wholesale was in the hands of syndicates that had a long-standing presence in California, such as Chinese, Italian or Jewish mafias, for instance. In those days, Mexican drugs had relatively restricted circulation: heroin was mainly used by war veterans, and marijuana was popular among Afro-American and Mexican youth, but not so much beyond that.

This changed in the 1960s, when the youth culture's glorification of marijuana and hallucinogens increased the market for Mexican marijuana. The Vietnam War also produced more customers for heroin. And the new youth culture as a whole developed an appetite for experimentation with new kinds of drugs.

I won't linger on the "Golden Age" of small-time drug running that accompanied the counterculture of the 1960s, with its occasional hippie-entrepreneurs and migrants paying for travel costs to the United States by transporting a kilo or two. This is a time that is remembered nostalgically in Mexico's traditional marijuana growing areas because markets were relatively open and peaceful then, and both production and distribution were small-scale, sometimes even occasional, business ventures. I wish instead to focus on the moment following those good times, when the production was consolidated, and distribution moved into the hands of professional organizations.

In California, this process of business concentration seems to have coincided in time with the multiplication of neighborhood gangs, whose numbers grew enormously from the 1970s forward, although the connection between the circulation of drugs and gang formation seems to have been indirect. Indeed, the formation of youth gangs in cities like Los Angeles tended to trace the ethnic and racial boundaries that exist in so many US cities, because they frequently began defensively in junior high schools that brought together youth from adjoining neighborhoods.

As a result, the social organization of Los Angeles's Mexican gangs (and, later, its Central American gangs) traditionally had only two levels, the level of the so-called *clica* (which is Spanglish for "clique"), which is made up of a small cohort of friends who hang out together, and a second level, which might be thought of as the neighborhood—or *mara*—level, which brings together all of the *clicas* in a neighborhood. Traditionally, the name of the neighborhood, or of the most representative streets of a neighborhood, is also the name of each gang. So, in LA there is the Avenues gang, El Sereno, Highland Park, Calle 18, and the Long Beach Longos, among others. A neighborhood gang's identifying signs are shared by all of its *clicas*: graffiti with the gang name or initials marks territories that belong to the entire gang, and gang members often tattoo letters, numbers, or icons that belong exclusively to them.

Ethnographic studies of Angeleno gangs carried out in the 1980s and 1990s described their social organization as being figured as a family of brothers, whose bonds are meant to be unbreakable, in particular, when it comes to confronting members of a rival neighborhood. At that time, too, gang leadership was unstable. So, for instance, in his study of one Mara Salvatrucha *clica*, ethnographer Thomas Ward characterized the reigning philosophy in the group as a kind of "democratic anarchy," with no fixed leader, and no obligations to follow orders.[6]

Nonetheless, the image of gangs as democratic organizations of sorts, which distinguish only between an "inside" and an "outside" and are characterized by violent rituals of induction, is to some degree "history." Today's gangs both are and are not exactly that. The gang originates as a defensive structure for a youth that is accosted by danger; but this youth has invented a way of life. The gang is at once an organ of protection and a lifestyle, characterized by a violent version of the sort of activity that we in Mexico know as *desmadre* (chaotic excess) and that California gang members dubbed *la vida loca* (the crazy life).

However, gangs are also organizations that are dedicated to extractive economic activities—extortion of local peddlers and merchants, for instance, or muggings—that derive from their control over streets and street corners. Journalist Tony Rafael reports an observation that exemplifies this aspect of gang economies in Los Angeles: "One Northeast vice cop could gauge the strength of Avenues influence in a neighborhood by counting the number of prostitutes on Figueroa Street. He said that when the taxation of prostitutes was in full force, the prostitutes would move on to other areas to avoid paying the rent. When Avenues was weak or off its game, the prostitutes would come back and work Figueroa again."[7]

Territorial control over streets and corners often allows gangs to participate in the drug retail business, which is the queen of illegal commerce in the United States. That participation can be direct or indirect. Gang members themselves can sell drugs on "their" corners, or they can charge rent to salesmen who wish to sell there. So, for example, a Tijuana-based organization of drug dealers known as "Border Brothers" built alliances with a number of Mexican-American gangs in LA, who charged them rent in exchange for being allowed to sell drugs on their corners.[8]

It is worth underlining that the neighborhood gangs have never had independent access to drugs, which is why they either charge rent for someone else to sell or else they make their own deals with wholesalers. In either case, there's a hierarchy between the person charging rent and the vendors on the corners, who are also the people running the highest risk of being caught by the police and spending time in jail. For this reason, even when a gang goes directly into drug retail in its neighborhood, the kids who sell on the corners have less prestige than the ones charging rent.

Sometimes there's an ethnic boundary between these two kinds of jobs. For example, LA gangs can be Chicanos, while their wholesalers can be Mexicans from Mexico. Anthropologist Fernando Montero explained to me that in a Philadelphia Puerto Rican neighborhood where he did extensive fieldwork on heroin use, the territory is not controlled by local gangs. The vendors on corners were all local neighborhood Puerto Ricans, but the "owners" of the corners—known as *bichotes*, a term combining the English "big shot" with the Puerto Rican *bicho*, meaning penis—are tough guys whose ethnicity varies from corner to corner. Wholesalers, for their part, are all Dominican.[9]

Territorial boundaries are fundamental for urban gangs in Southern California—lines separating neighborhoods, dividing avenues and streets, and, above all, corners are associated with gang ownership. Gangs reflect, reproduce, and reinforce an intricate system of demarcations, and they punctiliously differentiate between a territory's insiders and its outsiders. Often, gangsters mark their bodies with gang symbols as a kind of vow of unbreakable loyalty. These tattoos make them vulnerable when they are outside of their territory because they are an unequivocal mark of group filiation. The tattoos signal, then, an irrevocable profession of loyalty.

Given this rooted quality, it seems hard to explain how some gangs have acquired such strong translocal identities—for example, mega-gangs such as the Central American MS-13 or Barrio 18, or like the Bloods and the Crips in African American neighborhoods, or Chinese gangs that belong to the "Triad," or even white gangs of so-called Peckerwoods (of which there are fewer in Los Angeles) that are affiliated with the Aryan Brotherhood. If gang identity were exclusively a neighborhood thing and was founded in the intimate connections that develop in local *clicas*, how do mega-gangs manage to generate identification between youths who neither know one another, nor are from the same neighborhood, and who can even live in different countries altogether? The answer to this question is to be found in the prison system.

PRISON MAFIAS As the number of gangs and gang members rose—today, there are over 20,000 gangs in the United States and, according to the California Department of Justice, around 300,000 gang members in that state alone—the preoccupation with controlling them grew, and harsher punishments were slapped onto gang-related crimes. As a result, gang members generally suppose that sooner or later, they will do time in the US penitentiary system. This is especially so for those who sell drugs on corners, as well as for gangsters who participate in assaults or engage in a lot of street fighting. And this situation, in turn, has strengthened the connection between prison gangs and neighborhood gangs. In the case of Southern California, the Mexican Mafia, also known as La eMe, has ended up governing practically all ethnically Mexican and Central American gangs.

Created in 1957 as a way of defending Mexicans in California's state, federal, and juvenile prisons, La eMe initially called itself the Mexican Mafia because it was created shortly after the existence of the Cosa Nostra became widely publicized, when the police raided a boss meeting in the town of Apalachin, in upstate New York.

Thus, a small group of Mexican prisoners in San Quentin prison decided to create an organization inspired by the Italian mafia that, interestingly, was itself born in the prisons of Palermo and Naples in the eighteenth century. In California's prisons, however, racial identity was crucial, and, as I have argued elsewhere, the idea of a "Mexican race" itself emerged in the United States in the late nineteenth century, so that in mid-twentieth-century California, Mexican identity was seen and understood as being primarily racial.[10]

The Mexican Mafia thus saw itself as a champion of the "Mexican race" in California's prisons, a project that was then given concrete shape by La eMe's most famous ideologue, Rudolfo "Cheyenne" Cadena. Born in San Antonio, Texas, in 1943, and killed at the hands of the rival Nuestra Familia prison gang at the Chino, California, penitentiary in 1972, Cadena was an avid reader. According to journalist Tony Rafael, he was fond of Carlos Castaneda's esoteric books. In other words, he shared the Chicano movement's characteristic turn to *indigenismo*. Indeed, it was Cheyenne Cadena who first thought of renaming the organization La eMe, so as not to give itself a name that was in English and Sicilian (i.e., "Mexican Mafia"). He also was the one who thought up the idea of using the Aztec shield (*chimalli*) as the gang's tattoo, together with the letter *M* (for Mexico), and the number *13* (because the letter *m* is the thirteenth of the alphabet). Cadena also proposed the use of Nahuatl as a language with which to send secret messages (the way Navaho was used as code in World War II), despite the fact that Mexican prisoners who actually spoke Nahuatl were few and far between. He also began baptizing eMe members with the names of Aztec warriors. In other words, La eMe was founded as a Chicano secret society that identified, in its rituals, with the Aztec warrior caste.

In addition to such symbols, La eMe also set up strict rules of conduct for all imprisoned Mexicans: they all needed to keep themselves and their cells neat and clean, and they were expected to support all other members of their "race" and not allow any insult to "the race" to go unanswered.[11]

Apparently, the punctilious insistence on cleanliness as a marker of racial identity served above all to mark distances between Mexicans and African Americans, who La eMe portrayed as being dirty and promiscuous. The nineteenth-century Mexican prison term *mayate*, which evolved into a synomym of *puto* (roughly "homo" or "fag"), is still used by La eMe and its affiliated street gangs to refer to African Americans to such a degree that, in his book on La eMe, journalist Tony Rafael seems to believe that the term *mayate* is synonymous with "Black."[12]

After a few years, La eMe became the most powerful prison gang in the state of California, possibly due to the demographics of Mexicans in prisons, or maybe because of the identification between the Mexican Mafia and Mexico-based wholesalers ("the cartels"). We don't know. Even so, the rise of La eMe in California's prisons led to the exacerbation of racial antagonism among Los Angeles street gangs. La eMe has the Aryan Brotherhood as a junior ally—a prison gang that is a traditional rival of the Black Guerilla Family as well as the Nuestra Familia (also Mexican), which is the northern California counterpart—and enemy—of La eMe. Perhaps because of its rivalry with the Black Guerrilla Family prison gang, La eMe has at times monitored the internal racial composition of the neighborhoods that are run by Mexican or Central American gangs, and some years ago it even issued orders to empty those neighborhoods of any African American residents.[13]

Two things are relevant in all of this: first, that a racialized Mexican identity, capable of transcending rivalries between neighborhoods and *clicas*, flourished in the prison system, and second, that because most gangsters believe that they will one day go to jail, they also understand that they will one day be tributaries of a prison gang. This, indeed, is how La eMe began to charge street gangs rent even from prison: tributary street-gang members are protected when they go to jail. This, too, is the reason why orders to street gangs can be issued by prison gangs such as La eMe.

This articulation between prison gangs and street gangs adds a hierarchical tier to the latter that seems not to have been present among them in the 1990s, at least according to Ward's ethnography of a Los Angeles Mara street gang. Street gangs thus went from being "democratic anarchies" to organizations whose members have gone in and out of jails, have direct communication with La eMe, and aspire to be recruited as associates or even "made" members of that exclusive and powerful secret society.

Tony Rafael offers an anecdote that sheds light on that gangster upper crust: Alex, an eMe associate (not member) belonging to the Avenues street gang is in a car on a freeway with two other gang members, and they pass a car that is packed with members of a rival street gang. They begin "signing" to one another (making hand gestures that represent their gang). Almost immediately, Alex's two companions, one of them named Palomares, pull out guns and there is shooting between the two cars. And Rafael continues: "Alex was furious with Palomares. At this level of associates, the banging is expected to stop. Gang signs are supposed to be ignored, not challenged. At Alex's level, it's all about dope, money, taxes, kicking up to the big homies in prison, and regulating miscreants. Gangbanging is for the juveniles who still need to prove themselves by showing 'heart.'"[14]

Subordination to a prison gang thus gives rise to an internal hierarchy within the street gangs, whose more important figures are now charged with the business end of the operation. Subordination to the prison gang also allows street gangs to weave inter-neighborhood alliances and even for the gang's name to become an identity that transcends the neighborhood. The case of the Mara Salvatrucha, or MS-13, can serve as an example.

The Mara Salvatrucha began as a Salvadoran gang in Los Angeles. *Mara*, an abbreviation of *marabunta* (a swarm of ants, made popular in a Hollywood film), is also a metaphor for "the people" (*la gente*), the neighborhood (*el barrio*), or "gang." *Salva* is short for Salvadoran, and *trucha* is short for the imperative *ponte trucha*, meaning "heads up" or "wise up." The name therefore transmits an idea that we have already encountered: an ethnic or racial identity (*Salva*), a defensive function (*ponte trucha!*), and the idea that strength lies in neighborhood unity, in the *mara*. But when the *mareros* began filing through California's jails and prisons, they were dominated by La eMe, like all the other Southern California Mexican and Central American gang members.

This subjection manifested, in the first place, in a change of name: the Mara Salvatrucha became MS-13, with MS signifying

"Mara Salvatrucha," while the number *13* stands for the letter *M*, in other words, for La eMe. In prison, Salvadorans were thereby transformed into an ethnic satellite or subgroup of the "Mexican race," while they, for their part, gained prestige by way of ostentatious displays of violence. The combination of La eMe's validation, national pride, and ultraviolent methods allowed MS-13 to transcend identification with its original neighborhoods and include gangs operating in Salvador, Honduras, and Mexico, as well as on the East Coast of the United States.

From a spatial point of view, then, gangs have gone from being neighborhood organizations, composed of generational cohorts or *clicas*, to being articulated among themselves by way of the prison system. This development led to sharpened hierarchies inside the gangs—the difference between young street fighters and members who had been to prison—while gang territories started to be coordinated through prisons as networks of protection for the drug retail business. Thus, the Californian regional subsystem, which has its axis in drug retail, is organized from within the prison system, with prison gangs exercising ultimate territorial control. Taken as a whole, this regional subsystem therefore turns on rent extraction, collected in exchange for access to and protection over the main corners used for the drug retail business.

2. Regional Subsystem with Its Core in Drug Production (Prototype: Sinaloa)

The second subsystem that I wish to identify brings us back to Mexican territory, because we are now moving from an analysis of a portion of the drug economy that has retail at its heart to another whose elite is not composed of prison mafia members and their gang associates but rather of drug producers or, at least, of a rancher-*comprador* elite that has privileged access to farmers growing the product. This is a regional subsystem that originates in a rural elite that has woven connections with social actors including peasants, chemists, policemen, politicians, warehouse owners, and smugglers.

I use the example of Sinaloa state, in northwestern Mexico, as a prototype to discuss this kind of regional subsystem, recognizing that the regions that I use to figure these prototypes are always historically and geographically unique. My aim is to propose an ideal type that helps us understand the geography of Mexico's illicit (drug) economy as a whole and not to produce statistically representative examples of each regional subsystem.

It is true that in Mexico we know this particular type of subsystem—which has a rancher elite at its core—much better than we do the system that I just described for Southern California, which is based on the articulation between prison mafias and street gangs. Even so, a few notes about it are still in order.

The word *Sinaloa* has become something of a trademark, and the so-called Sinaloa Cartel is recognized throughout the world except, at times, in Sinaloa itself. Even so, it is worth noting that the core drug-producing region of Sinaloa is situated in the so-called Golden Triangle, which is a region that bridges parts of the states of Sinaloa, Chihuahua, and Durango. This is a key trait of Mexico's oldest and most famous crime organizations: they are rooted in a peripheral region that crosscuts several states.

This matters because no single state government can fully control the Golden Triangle's rancher elite. Indeed, cultural regions that thrive on the margins of various states regularly offer their elites ample room to maneuver both politically and financially. This is the case of the Golden Triangle, certainly, but also other well-known spaces for organized crime, such as the Tierra Caliente region that cuts through portions of the states of Michoacán, Guerrero, and the State of Mexico, as well as the isthmus region between Veracruz and Oaxaca, and the Huasteca area, whose territory cuts across the states of Hidalgo, Veracruz, San Luis Potosí, and Tamaulipas. All of these historical regions have been productive for local elites who are invested in illicit economies. In recent times, a similar logic also operates even in an industrialized region such as the Bajío, where gasoline theft has emerged as a major source of revenue for organized crime.

The original productive core in this sort of regional subsystem, on one side, lies in the connection between rural rancher-merchants who offer credit and protection to small marijuana and opium-poppy growers, and who in Sinaloa are known as *pesados* (men of weight), and on the other side, the peasant producers who are their suppliers. In order to make their product circulate, those same *pesados* rely on networks of politicians, policemen, soldiers, warehouse owners, chemists, accountants, and smugglers, often located in places that are distant from the sites of drug production.

ZONES A, B, AND C In spatial terms, this sort of region is built on the articulation between (1) a territorial "home turf," wherein property is fragmented, and there are numerous micro-producers who are socially and commercially rooted in so-called *ranchos* (hamlets), each of which is controlled by a strongman—the *pesado* or cacique—and is defended by that leader's gunmen, many of whom may be his kinsmen or dependents; (2) a municipal seat, in which a certain number of *pesados* congregate in order to govern the municipality, frequently as an agrarian oligarchy; and (3) the collection of all municipal seats of the productive region, whose elites are connected by kinship relations, alliances cemented through *compadrazgo* (ritual kinship), or by long-standing grudges between *pesados*, who identify with one another as members of an identifiable social class and subculture of *rancheros*. These three elements shape the core space of reproduction for this regional subsystem's dominant class. I shall refer to this core zone as "Zone A."

This sort of region may be controlled from a distance, if its elite has trustworthy stewards in place. Usually there are regional cities—frequently state capitals, but not necessarily—that operate at the very least as a seasonal productive and reproductive space for this elite. Such regional cities are used to concentrate, warehouse, and transport Zone A's (illegal) products; and they are also a destination for poor peasants and refugees fleeing the violence that is endemic to inter-ranch competition and to tensions with the military in Zone A. As a result, these regional cities are social centers where Zone A folks from a variety of backgrounds meet, and they can also be places where conflicts from Zone A are redeemed (either peacefully or violently), but also where new alliances can be forged. Finally, regional cities are useful places for pharmaceutical lab work in heroin production or, more recently, fentanyl or meth. After the internal market for drugs developed—a process that was deliberately avoided during most of Sinaloa's twentieth century—regional cities also became desirable markets in their own right, and so they have occasionally been tactical objectives that are fought over by competing warlords.

Regional cities are also the spaces in which Zone A's dominant class interacts with state political elites and with the state and federal police, as well as allies in the armed forces. Indeed, cities are critical for building political alliances, swelling one's numbers of dependents—hit men, scouts, couriers—and developing working relationships with a professional sector composed of chemists, lawyers, accountants, and personal service providers such as physicians. I shall call this segment of the regional economy "Zone B."

In the specific case of Sinaloa's class of heroin- and marijuana-peddling *pesados*, Zones A and B suffered violent military attacks during the 1970s so-called Operation Condor, when persecution, murder, and torture of participants in the drug trade reached such a pitch that *pesados* could not even operate out of their historic regional cities, including Culiacán, Mazatlán, and Los Mochis, and opted finally to move to Guadalajara, where they created the organization known as the Guadalajara Cartel, often considered the first major Mexican cartel. I won't discuss this development here, but it is worth noting that moving to an important capital that was not in any of the states crisscrossed by Zone A had organizational implications for the regional subsystem as a whole, since it displaced the regional elite, rooted it in a metropolitan culture, and thereby opened its horizons beyond the *pesados* traditional political connections, investments, and trade routes. In other words, government persecution of the drug trade made the geography of the productive regional system more complex.

Finally, this regional subsystem always requires articulation with international smugglers, many of whom traditionally resided near the US-Mexico border, and far from Sinaloa's Golden Triangle. I shall call those frontier regions that need to be controlled by the productive elite "Zone C." These frontier regions have always been a weak link for elites rooted in Zones A and B, because Mexico's productive regions are all far from the border, which means that the *pesados'* homegrown political networks may provide insufficient political protection there and force them to build up local political networks along the border. This circumstance explains why the smugglers who are the criminal elite in Zone C have at times felt tempted to overturn elites from Zone A, in particular when they no longer depend on their specific product, as occurred in the mid-1980s, when Mexico entered the cocaine trade. This was the moment when a number of powerful border cartels emerged, no longer seeing themselves as branches of Sinaloa producers, even in cases where the new head families hailed originally from Sinaloa, as was the case of the Tijuana Cartel under the Arellano Felixes or the Juárez Cartel of Amado Carrillo Fuentes, not to mention cases such as those of the Gulf Cartel in Matamoros, and later the Zetas, along the eastern (Tamaulipas) border with the United States, that heralded the rise of entirely new regional elites.

We can therefore think of this Zone C of the subsystem, which has drug production at its core, as a potential new Zone

A of another sort of regional subsystem, that has international smuggling at its core.

3. Regional Subsystem with a Smuggling Economy at the Core (Prototype: Matamoros, Tamaulipas)

The elite in this regional subsystem is neither made up of ranchers nor does it have its roots in the drug economy, but rather in the long history of smuggling across the US-Mexico border. In the first great era of Mexico's drug trade, before the arrival of Colombian cocaine, smugglers had three objectives: moving the product out of the regions where it was produced, which were often remote; reaching a strategic border area where they might be temporarily warehoused; and crossing the border to service wholesalers on the US side.

Since the later nineteenth-century, the development of Mexico's modern state had the border with the United States as its condition of possibility, and Mexico's political class profited from the regulation of international trade and the circulation of income generated through smuggling. There's nothing new about that. By the twentieth century, there were essentially two sorts of goods that were being smuggled: untaxed industrial products brought in illegally from the United States (known collectively in Mexico as *fayuca*) and illegal drugs flowing from Mexico into the United States. Because of the protective tariffs associated with import substitution industrialization, smuggling goods from the United States to Mexico dominated the border trade until the late 1980s. These included all sorts of industrial products, from refrigerators and toys to guns and candy bars. Every border city had its smugglers (*fayuqueros*). Smuggling was a business that did not trouble US authorities because products were generally purchased legally in the United States, but they did require developing a good working relationship with municipal and state police forces within Mexico, as well as with customs officers, highway police controls, and so forth. The most important capitals for this sort of smuggling were on Mexico's eastern border with the United States (from Ciudad Juárez to Matamoros), and especially the main ports of entry in the Tamaulipas-Texas border, most prominently Nuevo Laredo and Reynosa. This is because these towns were closest to the most important markets for the smuggled goods: Monterrey, Guadalajara, and Mexico City.

During the time when the Mexican drug economy was based on local production (marijuana and heroin), drug trafficking often moved through different routes than the great Tamaulipas smuggling route. The production centers of marijuana and opium poppy were mostly in the western Sierra Madre, and their most important market, California, was also on the western side. For this reason, the principal border towns for this traffic were west of Ciudad Juárez, with important points in Tijuana, Mexicali, and various towns on the Sonora-Arizona border. In short, before Mexico's involvement in cocaine, the most important (*fayuca*) smugglers were from the northeastern states of Tamaulipas, Nuevo León, and Coahuila, while the main drug-running border towns were in Chihuahua, Sonora, and Baja California.

Let us leave this initial conclusion in suspense for a moment—not forgotten—in order to take note of the fact that the *fayuca* market included one commodity that had a special status, which was the automobile. The illegal trade in American cars proved to be a useful bridge for eastern smugglers to transition into drug-running. Cars are a high-value product that is constantly visible on public thoroughfares. In order to sell smuggled cars for a living, the seller needs to be able to guarantee that the buyer shall be able to drive without facing constant police harassment. This means that smugglers need to be able to acquire license plates, registration papers, and sometimes even a fake vehicle identification number (VIN).

Such operations required good connections with the preventive police, as well as with the judicial and customs police, car agencies, and mechanics, a set of connections that also allowed smugglers to buy and sell stolen cars. The process of legalization for a used smuggled car, legally purchased in the United States, and for a stolen car was pretty much the same. So that the business of car smuggling was intimately connected to the business of stealing and reselling stolen cars.

When drug trafficking began to grow in scale and complexity, its reliance on car smugglers increased. It is said—I heard this in Culiacán—that several prominent traffickers made their start in the stolen car or smuggled car business, including Chapo Guzmán, Güero Palma, and Amado Carrillo. In his memoir, Nazario Moreno of Michoacán speaks of his participation in car smuggling in Laredo.[15] There is every indication that it was from this position that Nazario Moreno was recruited into the Zetas, from whom he later broke off in order to found the Familia Michoacana. Finally, there is the mid-twentieth-century Matamoros-based smuggling emporium associated with Juan N. Guerra, for whom stolen cars was a well-known branch of business and who developed excellent commercial and political connections on both sides of the border. His nephew, Juan García Abrego, was the founder of the Gulf Cartel, the first Mexican organization to transition into the cocaine trade. Mexico's eastern border was thus not initially specialized in drug trafficking, as was the case to a greater degree on the central and western borders, which were primarily controlled by Sinaloa traffickers and their partners in Chihuahua, Sonora, Durango, and Baja California Norte. This all changed when the cocaine trade began to course through Mexico.

That was the time when Juan García Abrego opened a route for the cocaine trade in partnership with the Cali Cartel; by 1993, he was Mexico's richest drug trafficker, according to Fortune Magazine. After his capture, García Abrego was succeeded by an equally prominent nephew, Osiel Cárdenas, who made the Gulf Cartel into the main rival of the Sinaloa syndicate. Cárdenas famously put together Los Zetas, a kind of Praetorian Guard, by hiring special-ops officers away from the Mexican army. It is thus no coincidence that eastern crime organizations quickly diversified the business away from an exclusive focus on drugs, and moved toward a generalized control of trafficking in the illicit economy. Given their background in smuggling, but having now benefited from windfall profits from the cocaine trade, the Zetas pursued the strategy of controlling *plazas* (a term used to refer to towns and municipalities), thus substituting the police in its function as regulator of informal commerce and local crime. They now sought to conquer and hold territories that would serve not only to transport drugs, but also to control human trafficking, and to extract rents like those the police had always levied, though with much greater voracity.

4. The Regional Subsystem with a Core in a Zone of Transit (Prototype: Honduras)

The fourth and final regional subsystem of the criminal economy that I wish to discuss again takes us outside of the Mexican territory, this time southward, but not to a major site of drug production, such as Colombia, whose criminal geography may have analogies to those of, say, Sinaloa, nor to the Caribbean Isles with major US-based populations, such as the Dominican Republic or Puerto Rico, whose role in smuggling may have similarities to the story we outlined for Tamaulipas. Instead, I wish to focus on a region that is dominated largely by Mexican crime organizations, though our government has never accepted any responsibility in this matter. These are territories of transit that can be controlled by those organizations. I'm referring specifically to Central America's so-called Northern Triangle (Guatemala, Salvador, and Honduras), a region that has been bitterly disputed by Mexico's most important crime organizations, particularly the Zetas, who for many years controlled Guatemala, and Sinaloa, who controlled Honduras. In recent years, the Cartel Jalisco Nueva Generación has jumped into the fray, but I shall not cover this development here.[16]

I shall focus my discussion on the case of Honduras, basing myself on a remarkable, though unfortunately still unpublished, study by Honduran anthropologist and journalist Tomás Ayuso, concerning the evolution of the rivalries between the MS-13 and Barrio 18 gangs there.[17]

In our previous discussion of the retail-based system found in California, I mentioned the birth of mega-gangs, which I interpreted as a result of the hardening of anti-gang legislation and policies. This led to an increase in gang members' circulation through the prison system. Among California's Central American gangs, this growth gave rise to a situation reminiscent of what students of kinship long called a moiety system, wherein an undetermined number of clans identify or distinguish themselves from one another in a bifurcated system, composed of two opposed halves (moieties). So, for instance, the Incan capital at Cuzco had twenty royal clans (*panacas*) that were divided equally into two moieties, associated with "upper" (Hanan) and "lower" (Hurin) Cuzco.[18]

Similarly, the hundreds of *clicas* and dozens of Central American neighborhood gangs of California grouped themselves in two competing organizations, MS-13 and Barrio 18, which are Central America's equivalent of Verona's Capulets and Montagues: wherever they find one another, they fight. In California, both of these mega-gangs pay rent to La eMe, and both learned a lot from that organization. They learned, for instance, that recourse to extreme violence and a politics of terror is effective when it comes to subjecting rivals, and that controlling prisons is a key to articulating locally rooted neighborhood gangs.

Tomás Ayuso begins his Honduran chronicle describing the moment when the Mara gangs were deported from California, in the 1990s, and tells how local Honduran gangs, petty thieves, and police were completely overwhelmed by the armaments and excessive violence that the *maras* routinely deployed. As a result, those local groups were either annihilated or subjected, and Barrio 18 and MS-13 quickly became the owners of the streets in Honduras's main cities.

Up to this point, the Honduran situation reproduces, to some degree, the situation found in California itself, where Central American gangs ended up attaching themselves either to MS-13 or Barrio 18, but there are also a few points of contrast. First, Central America's jails were not controlled by La eMe. And since members of Barrio 18 and MS-13 kill each other on sight, Honduran authorities preferred to keep them separate. This, added to the strong punitive measures adopted against *maras* by Central America's governments, in response to the terror that they have generated in the population, meant that the *mareros* were in a position to control local prisons, without paying tribute to La eMe.

The result of this was an intensification of the war between these two mega-gangs that reached extremes way beyond those encountered in the United States. Ayuso describes how the Honduran *maras* developed the strategy of forcibly evicting residents in order to create buffer zones between their neighborhoods and the areas controlled by the rival organization, such that there are entire streets in San Pedro Sula and Tegucigalpa whose houses lie abandoned. These empty buildings, known as *casas locas*—in a kind of sinister twist to the expression (*la vida loca*) that refers to the raucous lifestyle of LA's *clicas*—are places where *mareros* kill their enemies, keep hostages, and torture and rape victims. These houses are also where *mareros* train new recruits, and teach them how to be violent. "The people who end up in the *casas locas* have gravely inconvenienced the gang," writes Ayuso. "They are snitches, rivals from the other gang, people who they wish to blackmail, or police collaborators."[19]

The *maras*' imperium over the criminal and police element reached such an extreme that the whole of the urban geography is marked by them. Nevertheless, despite this degree of dominion, neither MS-13 nor Barrio 18 managed to transcend the business of extortion—the protection racket—in order to become, say, an organization like the Zetas or the Sinaloa Cartel, capable of controlling international drug trafficking through Honduras. This was due, Ayuso writes, to the fact that Honduran drug trafficking had long been in the hands of two rival "clans," the Valle Valles and the Cachiros, who were land-owning families at the head of private armies that had deals with the Sinaloa Cartel, which has donated large sums of money for political campaigns in Honduras over the years, as they are also known to do in Mexico.[20] The Sinaloa Cartel preferred not to deal directly with the *maras*, whom they viewed as being unreliable, just as the Zetas in Guatemala preferred to recruit local military personnel over *mareros*, for the same reason.[21] As a result, Barrio 18 and MS-13 battled fiercely for control of Honduras's streets, but their relationship to the drug market was limited to charging retailers rent or themselves to being the retailers. Just like in California.

However, in 2012 there was an interesting development: the Valle Valle and Cachiro clans declared war on one another and were so weakened as a result that the Sinaloa Cartel could no longer rely on them as intermediaries in the international drug trade, and was forced to opt for an alliance with MS-13—a partner they had nurtured in the United States to fight against the Juárez Cartel and the Zetas, and whom they considered less erratic than Barrio 18. As a result, MS-13 took a step up and became, for the first time, something more like a drug smuggling mafia and less like a network of neighborhood gangs.

The effect of this transformation has been that, whereas Barrio 18 has to engage in more and more extortion in order to keep up with MS-13, which is flush with cash, the Salvatruchas (MS-13) can now afford to adopt more benevolent policies and even engage in some redistribution of resources in the territories that they control. The entry of MS-13 into the wholesale trafficking business has made it less threatening to the ordinary citizen, whereas the lack of those connections makes Barrio 18 increasingly exploitative and feared.

A second effect has been that now local Honduran gangs (that is, with no California background) have started to challenge Barrio 18, and the moiety system that reigned for many years is beginning to break down, since MS-13 is no longer equal to Barrio 18, because of the strategic change in its role within this regional subsystem of the criminal economy.

Finally, MS-13 has also been expanding to the United States' Eastern Seaboard, where La eMe has no pull. It seems that, in this new area of colonization, orders to local MS-13-affiliated gangs come from prisons in El Salvador rather than from California's penitentiaries. However, it also seems to be the case that the Salvadoran prison elite has more difficulties disciplining affiliated gangs on the Eastern Seaboard than is the case of La eMe in California. It is logical that this would be so, because in California prison-gang control over street gangs is predicated on the expectation that all gangbangers will enter the prison system at one time or another. But MS-13's Salvadoran prison gangs don't control US prisons on the East Coast (at least not yet), and it seems likely that their capacity to impose policies, issue orders, or extract rent from faraway gang affiliates is irregular at best.

Conclusion

In this lecture I have showed how, rather than analyze one type of organization or another, it is more fruitful to study the rise and transformation of criminal organizations as part of an internally differentiated economic geography or, as G. William Skinner argued, as players in a regional system.

I explored four regional subsystems of the (transnational) drug economy. The first, anchored in retail, was explored through the example of Southern California, which is perhaps the richest and largest consumer market for illegal drugs. That subsystem is articulated by prison mafias, which in turn dominate neighborhood gangs. Neither type of organization, the prison mafia or the neighborhood gang, is specialized in wholesale, because they are neither producers nor specialists in smuggling illegal drugs out of Mexico and into the United States. Instead, they control the territory in which drugs will be sold; in other words, they either charge rent for retail or are themselves retailers.

The second subsystem, explained through the case of Sinaloa, originates with producers—campesinos and ranchers who, because their product is illegal, can never really become monopolists. Sinaloa is an oligarchy. There is no Sinaloan Jeff Bezos. Ownership there can never be concentrated in the hands of a single person or family. And when we speak of the Sinaloa Cartel, we are referring in the end to more or less durable, but essentially unstable, alliances between powerful players—Ismael "El Mayo" Zambada, the sons of Joaquín "El Chapo" Guzmán, Rafael Caro Quintero, the Beltrán Leyva brothers, and a long etcetera. This subsystem relies on complex political and commercial ties. Its most salient vulnerability has been that Mexico's traditional drugs—marijuana and opium—can't be cultivated near the US border, which means that producer organizations must control border crossings that are far from their natal territory. Their second point of vulnerability emerged with the introduction of three drugs that are not homegrown: cocaine, first, and then methamphetamines and fentanyl. This second factor strengthened the hand of a border smuggling elite, and gave rise to drawn-out wars for territorial control along the US-Mexico border.

I then introduced our third regional subsystem, exemplified by the case of Matamoros, home of the Gulf Cartel and eventually of Los Zetas. Those groups grew alongside cocaine trafficking—a complex business that involved reaching southward, to Colombia, as well as into the United States. The Gulf Cartel was supported in this process by its experience in smuggling products from the United States into Mexico, which was a business that required deep political connections, not only on both sides of the border itself, but also in Mexico City, Monterrey, Guadalajara, and other major inland cities. Although the Zetas were initially created as a military wing of the Gulf Cartel, their military logic, oriented to controlling territory rather than to moving products, proved highly effective as business diversified to include human trafficking, charging rent on drug retail sales within Mexico, engaging in gasoline theft, illegal logging, illegal mining or fishing, and more broadly charging for protection.

At a certain level, a parallel could be drawn between the Zetas modus operandi and California's prison mafias: neither had direct control over drug production. For this reason, the Zetas tried to gain control over the western state of Michoacán, which would have provided them with productive capabilities similar to those of Sinaloa, in addition to controlling a major port with intensive commerce to China (and so access to precursor drugs for meth and fentanyl production), but they lost control over Michoacán, and so concentrated on extending territorial control over an eastern corridor that went from Guatemala in the south to Tamaulipas in the north. The problem that they faced, however, was that they developed a strong reputation for relying too heavily on terror tactics and extortion. In this regard, the Zetas faced a quandary that, mutatis mutandis, has some parallels to the situation faced by Barrio 18 in Honduras: their heavy reliance on violence eventually made them into a target for the federal government.

The final regional subsystem that I identified, and discussed by way of the case of Honduras, has as its characteristic as being far from the United States, and not being a major drug-producing center, but being a useful area for transportation and resale. These are also spaces that have modest retail markets. Honduras is thus neither like Sinaloa (or Colombia), nor Matamoros (or Ciudad Juárez, or Nuevo Laredo, or Tijuana). Nonetheless, it is a region that is useful for Mexican and Colombian drug organizations, because cocaine can be purchased there more cheaply than in Mexico, and because none of Mexico's drug organizations has independent access to cocaine production. The result of this mix of factors is that the region ended up being dominated by mega-gangs, deported from California but operating under a more brutal system of extraction due to the comparative weakness of the Honduran state. The Honduran case also offers a glimpse of the process wherein a mega-gang can morph into a drug-wholesaler mafia and the effect that a change of this nature has on the dynamics of violence in the region.

5 Island of Rights, Sea of Extortion

O ver the past few decades, a new kind of state has been gestating in Mexico. It is characterized by heavy investments in sovereignty, understood here as autonomy of its central executive power, and by something close to an abdication of one of the traditional functions of the modern state, which is the regulation of policing and criminal justice. In this lecture, I delve further into this idea.

My argument shall be as follows: the seeds of the new state were planted during the context of the neoliberal reforms of the 1980s and 1990s, when a new economic space emerged. This space was governed according to criteria of legality and transparency that could be measured and judged outside of Mexico. Such a system would enable global financial markets, US and Canadian interest groups, and labor unions to have the information that they required to support commercial integration with Mexico. I refer to this rule-governed economic space as "the island of rights." It had been prefigured as early as the 1970s with the creation of a free trade zone that ran the length of the US-Mexico border, but the idea really took off with the proposal that Mexico would become a part of "North America," by way of a free-trade agreement—NAFTA, the North American Free Trade Agreement—which was promoted during the government of Carlos Salinas de Gortari (1988–94) and which finally came into effect on January 1, 1994.

Mexican promoters of NAFTA believed that NAFTA's regulations and rigorous procedures for certification and guaranteeing accountability would serve as a beachhead for the development of the rule of law, a condition that had never existed in Mexico's history. The implementation of the rule of law—albeit in the limited spaces of Mexico's new export-oriented economic platform—was, in fact, protected by the terms of NAFTA. Mexico's NAFTA enthusiasts wagered that transparency and equality before the law would spread beyond the confines of NAFTA-protected export industries and to other portions of Mexican society. The enclave of the rule of law was thus meant to grow in reach and extension, until one day it would provide legal coverage and protection for the entire country.

This ambitious project required deep reforms to Mexico's governmental infrastructure. For example, police reform was urgent because, as we saw in our second lecture, Mexico's system of policing relied on the systematic use of extortion, both for funding and as its enforcement strategy. During the era of Mexico's one-party rule, police extortion was tempered only by the limits placed on policemen by their superiors, usually in response to ad hoc requests from powerful politicians. Such a system was of course contrary to the very idea of the rule of law, where equal access to police protection and the equal application of rules is expected.

The fact that this violent and corrupt system of policing played an important regulatory role in the construction of the social order, and that it offered a measure of protection in cases or sites that had been singled out by politicians, was not immediately taken into consideration by Mexico's neoliberal reformers. What they saw and understood was that the NAFTA-sponsored "islands of rule of law" needed to count on a different kind of police force, less open to political clientelism, less reliant on bribery and extortion, more professional, and capable of protecting both citizens' rights and property rights. Rule of law requires a police force that does not rely on extortion as its main source of revenue. A total rehaul of Mexico's system of policing would thus be required.

However, the push for an ambitious reform of Mexico's system of policing competed with another equally urgent pressure, which was to preserve the mechanisms for regulating order in the ample sectors of the economy that were not up to the standards of code that were expected on the "island of rights," even though these sectors offered services that were important to keep the costs of Mexico's export economy down. Building a modern police force for the country required investments of the highest order—in sheer financial terms, certainly, but also in expert training and education. Given their mode of operation, Mexico's policemen were minimally educated (most did not even reach middle school), and training in police academies provided a socialization for cadets that was geared toward respecting internal hierarchies and understanding extortion practices.

In addition to its substantial price tag, reforming the police would also carry political costs, in particular, because reforms implied bringing new blood to the force—cadets with a high school education, for instance, or even with university degrees, and new mid- and high-level leadership. A shake-up in personnel disrupted preexisting relations of patronage. Moreover, if it was serious about extending the rule of law, the government would also need to modernize and strengthen the capabilities of its district attorneys' offices, courts, public prosecutors' offices, and prisons. Although neoliberal presidents from Ernesto Zedillo (1994–2000) onward acknowledged the need to intervene in those spaces, their efforts were inconsistent and important strategical mistakes were made, so that, by the time the war on drugs was declared in January 2006, government resources were already being channeled preferentially to the military rather than into repairing the justice system, and municipal police forces were increasingly neglected, while moves were made to bring the state and federal police under military command.

That situation has, if anything, worsened. The project of reforming the courts, DAs, prisons, and police has been scrapped, while the government has continued to pour more and more resources into what is by now rampant militarization.

It was the 2006 declaration of a war on drugs that closed the gestation period of Mexico's new state, which had been characterized up to that point by confidence in the idea that the rule of law would spread quickly beyond its NAFTA-protected beachhead. The decision to declare a war on the drug cartels was taken almost immediately after the 2006 presidential elections, when the losing candidate, Andrés Manuel López Obrador, challenged the validity of the elections and theatrically inaugurated a parallel, so-called legitimate, government, of which he was the "legitimate president." Having thus battered the credibility of the electoral process, confidence in extending the rule of law by consensual means sagged, and the government veered instead to further centralizing political power by declaring a national emergency of sorts: a war on drugs. That is when the formula "A lot of sovereignty, not much justice" began to take shape.

In addition to this political crisis, economic growth had not accelerated rapidly enough to formalize Mexico's enormous informal economy, and therefore didn't bring working conditions to the expected standards of the NAFTA isle. The policy measure that probably worked the most to help transform working conditions in the informal economy, designed by economist Santiago Levy and put into practice by health minister Julio Frenk, was to channel public investment in order to offer universal health care. Through the consolidation of that baseline of public well-being, the micro-family businesses that are prevalent in the informal economy could increase their productivity and progress toward integration with the economies and labor standards of the United States and Canada.

That policy made important strides—it was by no means a failure—but it was still a work in progress when the project was aborted during the current government of López Obrador, which slashed public health budgets after 2018 and dissolved the Seguro Popular program shortly before the COVID-19 crisis. This led to steep increases in medical expenditures, particularly among Mexico's poorest sectors. There ended the only consistent effort to formalize Mexico's economy.

In synthesis, rather than grow until it had extended its standards to the entire national economy, NAFTA and its protected businesses remained an archipelago within Mexico, with over half of the population working adjacent to it. This situation was further complicated by the exponential growth of the illicit economy that grew in tandem with the rest of the transnational economy. Its entrepreneurs took advantage of the deep recessions of the 1980s and 1990s and of Mexico's democratic transition to infiltrate legal business ventures and local politics. We already discussed this in lectures 3 and 4.

That is how the competition for political power between the two nodal sectors of the new economy—the formal sector and the informal sector—began, each with its most powerful segment deeply enmeshed in the transnational economy. Thus, there were the businesses involved in NAFTA on one side, and the so-called cartels, which are involved in the drug economy and in other legal and illegal businesses, on the other. This competition quickly moved into the political terrain to such an extent that by 2006 the government, that still championed the interests of the formal economy, launched its war against the cartels. That war was provoked, in no small degree, by the worrisome political influence that had been achieved by the illicit economy.

The rise in petty crime had been increasing since the mid-1980s, alongside the consolidation of organized crime, and this favored the sort of politics known as "punitive populism," wherein politicians and political parties campaign on platforms that favor building new prisons, tougher sentencing, and multiplying legal interdictions. Political grandstanding took precedence over finding ways to change Mexico's increasingly dysfunctional system of policing and overhauling its equally inadequate judicial system. Such projects were a lot more difficult to achieve than tougher sentencing laws, and less immediately effective from an electoral point of view. As a result, politicians of every political party preferred to cut corners, neglect costly and difficult reforms, and lean into punitive populism.

In addition to those unresolved challenges, the so-called war on drugs was launched without a close analysis either of the nature and size of the illicit economies that were being combatted, or of the implications that such a war would have on the previously existing system of security and justice. As a point of fact, the government did not have either the financial or the human resources to conduct a "war" while preserving its aim to extend rule of law. It lacked the institutional and the fiscal resources to do that. And it was precisely at the crossroads between a project of expansion of the rule of law through North American integration and a project of consolidation of internal control over the illicit economy by way of the military that Mexico's new state took its current form, governing with declared and undeclared states of exception, executed by the armed forces, with almost no capability to process malfeasance judicially. Inevitably, local policing fell under the control of organized crime and, as a result, governmental capacities to regulate the informal economy declined. And as the Mexican state lost its ability to regulate and oversee the operation of both informal and illicit economies, local and federal governments fell out of joint.

The transition from the early drug war moment of the new state to the regime that now calls itself the Fourth Transformation (i.e., the López Obrador presidency and the movement that it leads) is characterized by an inversion, a flipping over, of the government's most basic alliance: whereas earlier governments had represented the interests of the formal economy, that is, of the "island of the rule of law" that was built on NAFTA, the current government champions the interests of the informal economy, including the illicit economy. In this sense, the movement that pompously calls itself the Fourth Transformation—trying to stake a claim for a status that is comparable in significance to Mexico's independence movement, or to the social revolution of 1910–20—is in fact a much more modest "second transformation" of the state that was born out of the implementation of neoliberalism and North American integration. Indeed, the "first transformation" is what happened when the war on drugs was declared in 2006, a move that led to the neglect of the project of expanding the rule of law, particularly in regard to policing and criminal justice, in favor of imposing order by way of direct military action; and the "second transformation" (always lower case) is the one that is currently under way. It began when the political group that was aligned with the project of the "island of rights" lost control over local governance.

In Mexico's current phase, dominated by interests that represent economic sectors that are oriented to politicizing the economy rather than to securing property rights and reducing transaction costs, the government by no means seeks the abolition of the North American economy, because the informal and illicit economies that it represents have a relationship of codependence with it. Rather, Mexico's government uses its resources to augment pressure on the formal economy, and so widen the margins of negotiation between the formal and informal sectors, by applying political pressure on property relations, prices, and by increasing transaction costs. Mexico today is littered with roadblocks organized by various social movements, rife with organized criminal groups that charge rent for protection, street vendors demanding the right to expand territories, and so on. The Mexican state is now committed to repoliticizing the economy, against the ideal of the rule of law and self-regulating markets, in order to increase the political clout of the informal and illicit economies, as well as of a few allies among national entrepreneurs in the formal sector.

A corollary of these facts is that the differences between the state that began to develop under the neoliberal aegis and the current state do not turn on a left-right axis, as is often claimed, but rather on alternative uses of the state as an ally of the formal, export-oriented economy versus the informal and illicit economies. This does not imply that there are no active strands of the left and the right in Mexico—they certainly exist—but it does mean that left and right as traditionally understood do not accurately name the two opposing sides of the current divide, which has veered toward a form of identity politics marked by a polarity between the social classes that are culturally, educationally, or economically tied to local economies and those who are—again culturally, educationally, or economically—able to move freely in the formal spaces of North American integration.

Rather than a competition between left and right, ideological contention in the new state is anchored in alternative visions of the nation. One side sees Mexico's destiny as being tied to deep assimilation into North America and another sees government as the protector of a "people" who are territorially rooted in Mexico and who rely crucially on their ability to extract transaction costs from private investors. However, this polarity can obscure some of the shared interests between the two positions, because both parts need "the island of rights" to continue to exist—albeit with contrasting horizons of growth and well-being—and both need to guarantee some sort of status quo in the "sea of extortion" that surrounds "formal sector" investments. As a result, both favor the concentration of power in the presidency and militarization (albeit in different degrees and sometimes at cross-purposes), and both end up abandoning any serious attempt to reform the system of justice and policing, albeit—once again—for different strategic reasons.

The Problem of the Island

The idea that the transnational formal economy would serve as the rock on which the rule of law would be established always faced practical difficulties. We still don't have a documented history of what exactly happened in that regard; I am here proposing a reading of current events, as well as a set of questions, rather than a set of firm historical conclusions that are anchored in a thorough scholarly investigation.

The first question to raise concerning the dissemination of the rule of law on the basis of the regulatory apparatus introduced by NAFTA regards the relationship between Mexico's export-oriented businesses and their immediate physical surroundings. We know that these businesses were monitored internationally and had to conform to NAFTA's rules regarding the security of their property rights, access to supply chains and distribution, labor regime, and environmental standards, but what was the relationship between these businesses and the working environment that lay immediately beyond the industrial park?

Investments in Mexico's export-oriented manufacturing base grew astronomically with NAFTA, to the point that Mexico exports more manufactured goods than the rest of Latin America put together. These investments required training specialized and highly productive workers, but they also relied on keeping the cost of this labor force low, which could be done because worker reproduction relied on the services provided by Mexico's vast informal economy that provided workers with meals and domestic help and innumerable other services. Expanding investment thus did not imply uprooting the informal economy, any more than increasing the informal economy's leverage implies eliminating the export-led formal economy. These two economies are codependent.

At the same time, although NAFTA businesses also required a lot of public investment in transportation, schools, and urban services for their workers, private foreign investment was frequently enticed to this or that town by deals that allowed them to pay a minimum in taxes, at least for some years, so that the relationship between the "NAFTA island" and its immediate surroundings was not as immediately conducive to the extension of public goods, and to the extension of the rule of law, as one might suppose. The project that tied NAFTA to the consolidation of rule of law in Mexico presupposed that foreign investments would generate enough monetary spillover for the local tax base to grow and so, little by little, allow for the consolidation of proletarian residential neighborhoods that initially had been built under precarious and irregular conditions, often lacking paved roads, lighting, sewage, and other basic services. The hope—in the rare instances when it was explicitly formulated—was that the services that were in the hands of the informal sector would slowly be formalized as the residential areas around the factories consolidated their public services.

This idea was usually more of a tenet or belief than a conclusion based on hard-nosed economic calculations—since it depended on variables that were beyond the government's power to deliver. For instance, it was sensitive to the numbers of migrants who would arrive to try to find work in these new "poles of development," or to the actual number of businesses that would be attracted by the opportunities that were being granted to lure them in. Because growth under NAFTA was a wager, no firm calculation regarding the quality of public goods that would derive from direct foreign investment was truly possible.

As a result, the informal activities that flourished around Mexico's new industrial economy varied from place to place, but in no case was there an immediate and straightforward extension of the rights and work standards from the NAFTA isles to their informal suppliers. Indeed, a kind of apartheid developed, with a sharp contrast between the clear rules that governed the formal export economy and the consistent jockeying and negotiation that is required to manage the economy in its immediate surroundings.

Perhaps the most revealing expression of this tension, because it was the first to erupt in scandal, is the hundreds of unsolved femicides that occurred in Ciudad Juárez during the 1990s, which exposed the city's deeply insufficient investments in public lighting, transportation, policing, and housing for the women who worked in that city's assembly plants. The case also revealed a disconnect between Ciudad Juárez's export-manufacturing base and city governance. The assembly plants appeared to be insufficiently identified with their immediate surroundings: it was known that those factories could just as easily have set up shop in Ciudad Juárez, Tegucigalpa, or Guangzhou—and that they had chosen Juárez at least in part because of competitive tax arrangements. So, from the start, the new state was involuntarily generating images of the rule of law as an insular condition, surrounded by a society that was poorly policed, an economy that was poorly regulated, and a city that had to get by with insufficient public investment.

Codependency between the Island and Its Surroundings

At the same time that they began competing in the political arena, a codependency developed between the NAFTA islands and their immediate, predominantly informal, surroundings. Transnational corporations depended on the informal economy to cover some of their basic needs, while the cities that received them needed those businesses to provide jobs and opportunities to produce the spillover required for the upkeep of their entire population.

Beyond this, some formal-sector investors use their easy access to unregulated economies to access local resources that do not always have a legal provenance: access, for instance, to the exploitation of an aquifer for the operation of a mine, or to a sand mine that lies on community (*ejido*) lands. In such cases, those companies have often relied—directly or indirectly—on the intervention of armed groups or politicians who have ties to the illicit economy, in order to gain access to those resources. In these situations—which are common in Mexico's mining industries, as well as in the burgeoning export agribusiness—the connection between the NAFTA islands and their environs can lead to quite complicated arrangements around policing, combining reliance on private security firms that watch over the island with military surveillance over roads, while organized crime secures access to resources that are beyond the immediate reach of the company or guarantees safe passage to and from a mining facility.

Hybrid systems of protection and coercion have indeed multiplied in Mexico, combining municipal, state, or federal police, armed forces, private security firms, and armed units belonging to organized crime. These alliances are by nature unstable, since they are beholden to leaders who have conflicting interests. I have shown in the last three lectures that a political group that gains control over a municipal police force can be in conflict with the head of the state's police force or with the army officer in charge of the local military zone. Similarly, a company's private security firm may or may not find the support that it needs in local or state police, or in local, armed, organized crime. Indeed, criminal organizations can be unreliable for a variety of reasons, ranging from intergroup competition to lack of accountability; moreover, the armed organizations that are tied to the illicit economy generally try to diversify their portfolios and develop interests both in the licit and the illicit economy—drug trafficking or gasoline theft, for instance, wedded to legal transportation businesses, ranch ownership, or real-estate investments, so that the armed groups have too many chestnuts in the fire to become dependable partners.

As a result, the isle needs to develop a dense and heterogeneous network of local connections, and this implies engaging in constant negotiations—large and small—that are often marked by extortion and bribery or the application of political pressure. This field of negotiation pertains to what I call the "sea of extortion," although the appellation is perhaps too simplistic and maybe also too dramatic, since many of these negotiations do not quite reach the terrain of extortion, though they do always transpire with the *possibility* of extortion as a backdrop, since negotiations occur with the understanding that the rule of law does not extend to the economies in question, and therefore that recourse to public force and the justice system, too, must be negotiated.

The Logic of Polarization

One of Ernesto Laclau's most frequently cited ideas regarding populism as a political logic is that populism—that is, politics based on dividing society between "the people" and an "anti-people"—generates consensuses that are unstable with regard to their specific content, since the figure of the leader, who is essential to this political form, functions as an "empty signifier," whose programs vary according to the nature of the coalitions supporting him, and subsequently to the ways in which his adversaries—the anti-people—are defined. For this reason, again in LaClau's view, populism can be adopted by the right or the left, and it can be either a progressive or a regressive force.[1]

I'm not interested in the debate on what is and what is not populism, or what its characteristics are. My concern is both more modest and more specific: I wish to characterize a new state that has emerged in Mexico. In order to achieve that aim I take a path that runs contrary to LaClau's pursuit of a "political logic." Instead, I wish to identify the substantive class dynamics that define and mark the limits of the new state.

The political form that we call populism has an intrinsic relationship to democracy, since democracy is characterized by a latent tension between the institutional management of the state and the very notion of popular sovereignty, which is anchored in an ideal of universal suffrage. This tension between the will of the people and the work of the state is the condition of possibility for the emergence of a leader who represents— or claims to represent—the majority against the institutions of the state and its established modes of representation. It is a kind of tension that can be found in ancient Rome as well as in twenty-first-century Argentina. Here I am interested in something else.

The new state in Mexico began to gestate after the 1982 fiscal crisis and the institutional reforms promoted by the International Monetary Fund that were unleashed as a result. Today, this new state is governed by a populist president, but its characteristics transcend the liberalism/populism duality, even though there are tangible and significant differences between those two political alternatives: they are in fact antithetical manifestations of a single process of state formation.

The 1982 debt crisis abruptly closed the era of import substitution industrialization as Mexico's development strategy, and the country's turn to free trade and neoliberalism presented the Mexican state with both a challenge and a promise. The challenge was that it had to restrict the scope and application of some of its traditional practices of political control, such as, for instance, the corporativist organization of political society that since the 1930s had been organized around the social classes that were pillars of the official party. The government also had to relinquish its monopoly over the legitimate politicization of the economy, which had until then been accomplished through the extraction of tribute—what we today call "corruption"—in exchange for guaranteeing the operation of the market.

155

This created serious political difficulties for both the government and the official party, foreclosing any possibility of continuing to govern with the single-party, presidentialist system that Mexico had managed to sustain since 1929. In short, the economic crisis of 1982 also generated a political crisis. But Mexico's transition to a neoliberal economy also presented reformers with an opportunity, which was finally to promote a viable route for the installation of the rule of law, understood as a system wherein all persons and institutions are accountable to laws that are equally enforced. This route gained traction thanks to NAFTA, a treaty that emplaced the rule of law in a number of areas of Mexican life.

So, although neoliberalism provoked a major crisis of governability, laying the way for the collapse of a regime that had been in place for the better part of the twentieth century, it also opened up a new horizon that had its own sources of support and popularity: the achievement of the rule of law. That goal served to justify no end of more or less sound, more or less improvised, policies and institutions. And it was used to alleviate the political pressure that came from sectors working outside of the NAFTA island, where lives were being affected, sometimes gravely, by the deep social and economic changes that free trade wrought.

The government faced two big challenges, then: it needed to design a workable system of representation and control—since the earlier one could not continue functioning under the new economy—and it had to extend the island of the rule of law beyond the formal export economy to which it was initially tied. It is in this dialectic, this tension between the need for order and the goal of expanding the rule of law, that Mexico's new state began to take shape.

In its early stage (late 1980s to early 2000s), Mexico's reformers had no intention of neglecting the country's policing and criminal justice system, but rather the opposite: they sought to change the system so that the police and the courts might stand as guarantors of equal access to the law. The physiognomy of the new Mexican state is a story of the defeat of the project of achieving the rule of law for the country as a whole. That story has the 2006 drug war as a key turning point.

The Failure of National (Elite) Pacts

Given the challenges that the old political class faced, Mexico's transition to democracy turned quickly to the idea of a national pact, based on agreements between signal members of various elites, as a useful—perhaps indispensable—mechanism to transition from a hegemonic, one-party state to a democratic government with institutions capable of implementing the impartial application of the law. This sort of compact seemed necessary to lend credibility to new institutions: only if they were recognized by the country's most widely respected personages might they be trusted. Instead of being run by members of the old political class, and rather than relying on the informal mediation of traditional caciques, the state's new democratic institutions would need to be autonomous, and they would be placed in the hands of exemplary citizens, whose personal reputations were beyond question.

Mexico's democratic transition thus leaned on two related strategies. The first was to seek agreements between leaders of varied—and sometimes opposed—interest groups, by way of creating fora that allowed those leaders to speak freely among themselves, gain some trust, and arrive at shared principles for governance. This was tried on several occasions, beginning perhaps with President Miguel de la Madrid's Pacto de Solidaridad Económica, which brought together labor and business leaders to agree on how to distribute the hardships that came with the deep recession and hyperinflation of the 1980s; the Grupo San Angel was organized a dozen years later to facilitate the transition away from control of the presidency by the Partido Revolucionario Institucional (PRI); and, more recently, the Pacto por México sought to establish ground rules between three main political parties, geared toward strengthening the state in exchange for establishing various political concessions to each. These initiatives, and others like them, brought together prominent politicians of different persuasions, opinion leaders, media tycoons, intellectuals and journalists, union leaders, captains of industry, and other weighty figures with the idea of finding common ground toward a modern system of political parties, reliable elections, and the consolidation of a democratic institutional framework.

Curiously, the effort to create what liberals refer to as a "level playing field" thereby relied on an antiquated, nineteenth-century sort of figure—the *notable*—who, in Mexico, still held some sway. The notable is a person with a well-known name, whose honorability is everywhere recognized. Often notables come from important families. Usually these people—whom the press frequently refers to with the prefix *don* (or *doña*) or sometimes as *maestro*, in the case of prominent artists or intellectuals—are prominent members of the liberal professions, artists, well-known university professors, or valiant leaders of civil society. Occasionally they may be politicians who have risen above the drab rituals of submission characteristic of the one-party system.

These notables, together with captains of industry, politicians, and union leaders, were brought together in a kind of Parnassus, where they acknowledged their differences and worked to reach agreements that would help transition Mexican political society peacefully, while guaranteeing spaces and concessions to each sector. Nevertheless, this social imaginary— the idea of a summit agreement—necessarily left out many prominent leaders of the illicit and informal economies. There were no leaders of taxi driver associations or market vendors, captains of organized crime or leaders of peasant villages, whose livelihood was being undermined by free trade. As a result, while the notables' agreements flooded the opinion pages of Mexico City's papers, the summits as a whole were detached from organizations that were taking shape in response to dire circumstances, or from the substantial illegal opportunities that were presented by the new economy. Ironically, this process ended up destroying the notable as a politically relevant figure, since the notables' influence depended, in the end, on a courtly logic that was still operational in the neobaroque mannerisms of the old PRI era. This logic crumbled with the arrival of new economic elites and, more broadly, with the values that came hand in glove with the new economy. Eventually, even the republic's presidents began neglecting the deference that they'd once extended to this estate of notables. Every day they felt less compelled to be close to them, or to the high culture that was that estate's most rarefied possession.

It is true that the system of notables appeared to have been reanimated after the 2018 ascension of Andrés Manuel López Obrador to the presidency. López Obrador's obsession with inscribing his name in the great hall of Mexican Patriotic History had as a natural consequence an almost irrepressible attraction for surrounding himself with people with last names imbued with the aura of history. Thus, López Obrador appointed a Vasconcelos here, a Cárdenas there, and a Scherer over there; or perhaps a descendant of a revolutionary leader like as Antonio Díaz Soto y Gama, or one of the few remaining historic leaders of the '68 student movement, or the daughter of a well-known victim of Mexico's Dirty War of the 1970s. López Obrador's cabinet and his congress are speckled with descendants of historic personages. However, the president did all of this not to guarantee the legitimacy of his governing institutions but rather to endow his personal image with the gravitas of History (with a capital *H*), manifested in the presence of the remaining descendants of History's protagonists. López Obrador needed this to become not just a sitting president but a leader who, like King Arthur, identifies his own body with the body of the nation; for, as López Obrador declared on the night when he finally won the national elections, "I no longer belong to myself."

The notables' influence subsequently went into a tailspin—as they transitioned from being autonomous actors, members of a kind of aristocracy, to being the subordinates and employees of the president. They were now used principally for an ornamental, liturgical purpose, and their ability to protect even their honor was often worn down by bots, memes, and tweets, including the anonymous and gratuitous vilification that characterizes public exposure in the digital era. And as the notables, who had existed for two hundred years, went down the road of extinction, so too did the idea that the country could be governed by way of a summit agreement.

What developed instead was a strategy that relies on polarization to organize the political field. Polarization turns on two alternative camps: the champions of a rule of law that is in line with international treaties, standards, and global objectives, including human rights and environmental objectives, and that is anchored in a globalized (formal) economy, versus the sectors that favor the politicization of the economy, making it sensitive to brokerage and negotiation within a nationalist frame that is (ideally, though not necessarily) orchestrated by the government. In other words, the central contradiction in Mexico appears to be organized around those who would use nationalism to further what Karl Polanyi called a socially "embedded" economy—which is a position that has at its heart informal and illicit economic activities that always need to be negotiated in order to exist, but that also involves the ambition to gain direct control over government jobs and revenue—against sectors that prefer to strengthen the rule of law by way of deeper cultural, economic, and political imbrication in a globalized sphere, a position that has cultural implications, too, since it requires moving beyond—if not outside—the national frame.

161

What is interesting about this polarity is that neither side has any real possibility of eradicating the other. So, for instance, the language of human rights and the rule of law is a recourse for the entire political spectrum by this point, with no exceptions, while the clientelist, ad hoc negotiation of concessions—beyond any a priori rights—is an equally quotidian and universal practice.

Finally, it is worth noting that the competition between a formal globalized economy that is anchored in internationally monitored rules and a local economy that favors political intervention in markets does not correspond to contradictions, à la Marx, between capital and labor. The informal and formal economies are, as we have seen, codependent, and each has its own workers, entrepreneurs, and political elites. A country that is as complex as Mexico can be ruled neither for the formal nor for the informal sector. For that reason, the current government does not actually seek to bury the NAFTA "island" (rebaptized in 2018 as the T-MEC island, for the Tratado entre

México, Estados Unidos y Canadá). On the contrary, López Obrador fought tooth and nail to renew the trade accord—even agreeing, in order to secure US approval, to dedicate thousands of troops to catching Central American migrants and keeping them out of the United States.

Suspicious Truths

In my second lecture I described how the Mexican state became estranged from its institutions of criminal justice. That estrangement occurred in part because of the uncoupling of the local police corps and the institutions that they're meant to coordinate with, a situation that has led to conflict—sometimes even armed conflict—between municipal and state police forces, between state and federal forces, or between police and the military. This disarticulation between police institutions makes it hard to reach credible judicial resolutions even in emblematic cases, such as the case of the forty-three Ayotzinapa students, or the case of two mass graves for murdered and tortured people that belong to the state of Morelos's attorney general's office in the towns of Tetelcingo and Jojutla, or the massacre of seventy-two and then of almost two hundred additional Central American immigrants in San Fernando, Tamaulipas, or the thirty-five presumed Zetas who were beheaded in the port of Veracruz, or the thirteen police officers who were recently murdered in the town of Coatepec de Harinas, or the eight state police officers who were ambushed and killed in the town of Aguilla, Michoacán, a couple of years ago, or the twenty-eight inmates who were killed in an uprising in the Acapulco prison in 2017, or the fifty prisoners who were killed in the Topo Chico penitentiary in Monterrey in 2016, or...or...or...the list of unsolved "emblematic cases" goes on and on. No scandal is big enough to ensure that justice will be served.

Indeed, it is surprisingly difficult to produce a broadly shared view of the truth in any one of these cases or in any other case like them. This is due not only to insufficient investments in the justice system—in professionalization of forensic experts, training police investigators, and so on—but also to lack of coordination between various institutional authorities, or even to open conflicts between them. Thus the Enrique Peña Nieto government spent copious amounts of money to establish what they pronounced as the "Historical Truth" of the forty-three disappeared students in the Ayotzinapa case, but even their thousand-page report did not succeed in establishing a widely believed version. The López Obrador government, which has continued to invest profusely and disproportionately in this particular case, has also failed to produce a socially accepted truth or to execute justice. This is because, in matters of criminal justice, the new Mexican state no longer has the capacity to establish truths that can be generally believed, because it lacks a judicial system—judges, district attorneys, investigative police, forensic experts—that is sufficiently professional, trusted, and well-funded for its results to be credible.

The effects of this are sorely felt by anyone seeking justice, as can be ascertained by the aforementioned example of the mass graves found in the towns of Jojutla and Tetelcingo, in the state of Morelos. Those graves are in municipal graveyards, in sections that belong to the attorney general of the state of Morelos, and they were supposed to be used for the interment of unclaimed, duly and legally processed corpses. Thanks to the work of family members of victims of forced disappearance in the region, however, it turned out that these graves had been used instead to inter literally hundreds of murdered, tortured, and unregistered bodies (at least 211 have been discovered so far, though there is a section of the Jojutla burial site that has not yet been excavated, where more remains are believed to be buried). The collectives of the families of the disappeared of the state of Morelos have not stopped demanding a convincing investigation of the case, which has not yet happened. The federal prosecutor has refused to take the case on, so Morelos's attorney general is supposed to lead an investigation into the dysfunctionality or criminal complicity of his own office.

In such a context, the organizations of family members of the disappeared do not trust *any* governmental institution with the work of DNA identification of the bodies. Rather, they demanded that four different institutions carry out separate, independent DNA tests, and that they then cross-check results between them to be sure that a positive ID could be credibly established for each victim. In other words, the families of the victims are convinced—thanks to their previous experiences—that there is no government institution that can be trusted with the process of DNA identification of the presumed victims of organized crime. In Mexico's new state, governments have forfeited their power to establish any credible version of the truth when it comes to criminal justice, and this incapacity to create a shared truth has in its turn led to the creation of a new set of state rituals. I shall conclude today's lecture with a brief note in this regard.

Rituals of the New State

In my introductory lecture I referred to David Graeber and Marshall Sahlins' remarks on the advisability of analyzing sovereign acts and the sacralization of sovereign power separately. The acts through which sovereignty is established—the acts of the founder of a royal dynasty, for instance—are, as a rule, extraordinarily violent, both materially and symbolically. They frequently include acts of incest, fratricide, parricide—that is how kings are recognized and kingdoms are established. This is because the sovereign is always an extraneous force with respect to the customary order; violence is used to demonstrate this eccentricity or, more precisely, to invade and overwhelm the customary order. This externality of sovereignty is what makes kings sacred beings, separate from everyone and therefore capable of judging others. Indeed, Graeber and Sahlins claim that "the monstruous and violent nature of the king is an essential condition of his sovereignty."[2]

Societies develop rituals that serve to tame the unpredictable violence of the king and to attenuate his propensity for violence. This argument has some kinship with another, developed by Moshe Halbertal in his discussion of sacrifice in monotheism. For Halbertal, sacrifice is different from a normal gift because there is an unbreachable distance between the condition of the sacrificer and that of God, so that no offering, no sacrifice, is capable of compelling God to do anything. That is the frightful lesson of the story of Abel and Cain, who sacrificed the products of their labor to God. The shepherd Abel sacrificed a ram, while the farmer Cain offered the fruits of the earth. And God accepted Abel's sacrifice, but he rejected Cain's. Why? We cannot know. Halbertal argues that this uncertainty—the anxiety of not knowing whether one's sacrifice will be accepted or rejected by God—leads to obsessive ritualization. The logic, simply, is that if sacrifices are carried out in highly standardized, punctiliously ritualized ways, the likelihood of their being accepted increases because, in principle, there would be no difference between sacrifice A, sacrifice B, and sacrifice C. People fear sovereigns because they are inherently unpredictable and because of the lack of any true reciprocity between themselves and their sovereign. This infuses even willful submission with a degree of fear and uncertainty.[3]

When he was inaugurated as president, López Obrador declared, "I no longer owe myself to me." The apparent meaning of this statement—which has often been repeated since—is that the president's life is now owed to the people, who are the source of his power. However, there is also a second implied meaning, which is that, because López Obrador is no longer attentive to his own interests, he is different from everyone else. He is no longer self-interested and is therefore set apart from society; it is from this place of separation that he might judge even his own kin if they were proven to be corrupt (or so he claimed). The president can carry out violent acts of sovereignty, because he is outside of the "social fabric." He is not an interested party. He does not own himself but is owned instead by a metaphysical entity (the people).

This exteriority with regard to the social fabric inspires fear, because it is a place from which violence can be exerted, and so the president's entourage ritualizes its interactions with the president with panegyrics and loyalty oaths, forms and formalities, to try to appease or mollify him. The president's words and gestures therefore become the subject of punctilious, daily exegesis. This is sacralization at work, and the new Mexican state—both in the period led by the champions of the island and in the period when it is championed by an ally of local and informal economies—has developed those characteristic new rituals, in the face of the violence that presidents can let loose.

Criminalization of the Victims

The first sacralizing ritual of Mexico's sovereign power was the criminalization of the victims of violence. This strategy was initially developed during the presidency of Felipe Calderón, though it is still a part of the official arsenal today. It consists of separating the victims of violence from the rest of the nation to such a degree that the dead or the disappeared can be treated as if they were nationless or, to put it another way, as if they were not members of the same political community.

This strategy of blaming the victims, and separating them from the political community, was also used to sacralize the violence of the sovereign, since the armed forces are identified as coexistent with sovereign justice. The armed forces have the president as their commander in chief, and through them the sovereign is identified as the provider of a kind of justice that rises above the courts. The violence of the state becomes sacralized as a purified violence, capable of transcending petty or corrupted institutions such as the police or the courts, or as a form of transcendental—quasi-divine—justice.

As a popular supplement to this ritual, which serves to purify the violence of the state, other rituals and symbols were developed by criminal organizations that served to indicate the kind of identification they sought with that very same fetishized state. The instability of these identities is of crucial importance. So, for instance, there are some militias that (1) seek to be seen as one with the people, or (2) flaunt symbols of class or even caste distinction with regard to the lower folk in their communities, or (3) develop in a mimetic relationship with the armed forces. Thus, when the army enters towns that are under the power of a cartel, there have at times been popular protests against this "outside intervention," often with women and children in the front lines bearing signs and banners as if in a spontaneous expression of popular rejection. Such protests are often orchestrated—it is known—by the cartels themselves, whose members blend in with the populace and stand in opposition to the army. In such situations, "organized crime" presents itself as being *one with the people*, and it presents the army with a situation wherein fighting the cartel might well imply fighting the people.

There are other occasions when criminal organizations adopt all of the trappings of the military, wearing modern military uniforms with the insignia of their cartel, using tactical military equipment, riding on monogrammed vehicles that bear the insignia of the cartel, and so on. In such cases, the cartel seeks to communicate that they are capable of acting responsibly, predictably, and in a visible manner, just like the state. To the

168

government, they are saying that the territory that they occupy belongs to them.

These swings in strategy concerning cartel identification perform the alternative sort of situation that organized crime seeks to establish vis-à-vis the state. In some instances, organizations want to be confused with "the people"; in others, they prefer to be recognized as a local or regionally dominant oligarchy, a new class of big men; and in yet others, they are at pains to appear as an organized, state-like, bureaucratic force that is capable of enforcing an impersonal and predictable order in the towns that the cartel occupies.

In the new Mexican state both "society" and "the state" thus live in fear of having been "infiltrated" by organized crime, and so there is a deep current of anxiety with regard to the cohesion of the *community*, as much as there are obsessions with regard to the integrity of the *state*. Sometimes this complicated politics of identification is reflected in the names that criminal organizations give themselves, which oscillate between corporate images, such as La Empresa, Cartel del Milenio, and Cartel del Golfo, and communitarian sorts of images, such as La Familia Michoacana or Unión Tepito. Just as the new state is haunted by the suspicion that the crowd that presents itself as "the people" may perhaps not be speaking for the people but rather for the private interests of organized crime, so too are communities sometimes unsure of whether local armed groups are their protectors or their invaders. The new state is thus characterized by blurred lines between the illicit economy, society, and the government.

6 Contingency as the New Zeitgeist

The Era of Contingency

In January 2014, I published an op-ed in *La Jornada* on the rise of Michoacán's *autodefensa* movement, a grassroots uprising against the oppressive domain of the Knights Templar drug cartel. In it, I argued that there is a recurring tension between social organizations inspired by a military model and those that appeal to the family as an organizational model. The idea that I had back then, and that I explored in some depth in a case study that I published about a police raid on a hospice for street children known as La Gran Familia, was that in Michoacán there was a kind of recursive or oscillatory movement between strategies of territorial control inspired in bureaucratic, vertical, rationalized organizations that have the army as their prototype, and control strategies that appeal to community-based or familial paradigms.[1]

I also concluded that the tension between a model founded in the image of rational bureaucracy and another built on familial power is characteristic not only of organized crime but also of governmental institutions, as we have seen in lectures 2 and

3 on the organization of Mexico's police. In Michoacán, criminal organizations oscillated between making appeals to family and community (giving themselves names such as La Familia Michoacana or Los Caballeros Templarios—guardians of morality and religion—or Autodefensas Comunitarias) and adhering instead to a corporate and bureaucratic model, instantiated in organizations such as Los Zetas and, more recently, the Cartel Jalisco Nueva Generación, which have adopted the military model. We can find similar tensions within the government itself, where the chain of command and responsibility is often

melted into the molasses of kinship and friendship, with rhetoric oscillating between claims for the rule of law and appeals to communitarian identity. The pendulum swings between appeals for rational bureaucratic (and meritocratic) organization and communitarian morale are an expression of the tension between formal and informal economies.

I will now build on this idea in order to explore its societal implications. To the extent that the project of mooring the rule of law in international regulations has either failed or proved to be insufficient, Mexico's institutional order is structurally unstable. As a result, state institutions appeal alternatively to the principles that are central to the operation of the informal economy—for instance, trust and intimacy (*confianza*), loyalty, godparenthood, brotherhood, and so on—or to a rational-bureaucratic scheme, where appeals are made to respect rank, chains of command, discipline, principles of legal equality, and so forth. In this final lecture, I focus on the cultural and ideological implications of the instability and the constant oscillation between these two organizational models.

The instability of both the familial and the governmental orders is a characteristic of Mexico's new state and of the political
economy that gave rise to it. Even so, the constant oscillation
between appeals to family and to rule of law did not find a to-
temic sign until the 2020 COVID-19 pandemic, when the term
La Contingencia (The Contingency) became ubiquitous. The
practical implications of The Contingency, written with capital
letters, condense the cultural politics of this new era because
the term names a strategy of governance that has been central
to the new state, while it also resonates with microlevel familial
strategies. This is why The Contingency expresses the spirit of
the times—and it can serve to name today's zeitgeist—as much
as *La Crisis* (The Crisis) summed up the spirit of the times in
Mexico's 1980s and 1990s. This lecture explores one avenue of
research into the zeitgeist, by way of an analysis of family reproduction strategies.

Exit, Voice, Loyalty, Hedging

In 1970 Albert Hirschman published his famous essay on exit,
voice, and loyalty, where he discussed the alternatives that social actors face when they confront deteriorating institutions.[2]
His ideas are a useful starting point for us because our era has
been marked by the deterioration or decline of entire ways
of life—that of the peasantry, for example—and by the bank-
ruptcy or restructuring of various branches of activity. This
accelerated process of "destructive creation," as Joseph Schum-
peter famously characterized capitalism, is at the heart of the
sociology that I wish to explore.

Hirschman said that in the face of institutional decay, social actors face a dilemma: to abandon the institution, to try to change it through increased participation, or to remain loyal to it (warts and all). Hirschman summarized the first option in his concept of *exit*, the second with the term *voice*, and the third with that of *loyalty*. Hirschman's third concept, loyalty, influences the decision of whether or not to jump ship, when such a choice exists, but also the ways in which a social actor speaks out. A person who chooses to emigrate can be seen as a traitor— as used to happen in Mexico during the 1950s and 1960s, when migrants to the United States were portrayed as disloyal to their country (and disparagingly referred to as *malinchistas* or *pochos*). The same person can be thought of as having had the courage to explore better opportunities, as happened during the presidency of Vicente Fox, who declared that "it is the best who leave," or as happens today, when Mexico's current president, Andrés Manuel López Obrador, calls these same migrants "national heroes," provided that they (we) continue to send remittances back to Mexico. Hirschman's classic thesis is useful, then, not only for analyzing the decisions of, for example, corporate employees or parents in the face of the deterioration of public schools, but also for understanding how migratory decisions are thought of and made. And it will also serve us in our analysis of the rise of *contingency* as a sign of the times, albeit with one important amendment.

When discussing family strategies in the face of reproductive crises, a fourth option needs to be added to Hirschman's dilemma between exit, loyalty, and voice. It is an alternative that has gained so much ground in economic life that it has been formalized in the world of finance with the concept of *hedging*, which refers to a strategy based on a risk calculation. Actors try to reduce the prospect of losses of an investment by diversifying their "portfolios" in such a way that if one of their bets loses out, there will be another that wins, preventing any catastrophic loss.[3]

This sort of calculus also occurs in social and political life, of course, and not only at the level of individual strategy but also at the family and even community level. This is where I am going to concentrate my attention. A peasant family that depends overwhelmingly on remittances sent from abroad by one of its members plants a cornfield in case its migrant member loses her job or suffers an accident. A university professor loses his quality health insurance because of a new government policy but decides against opting out of academia. Nor does he choose to exercise his voice of protest, not because he thinks that if he maintains discipline things at work will one day improve, but rather because the faculty position may facilitate landing the odd job in government consultancy that can cover a part of his loss.

Here I intend to explore the kinds of alternatives that have been recurring family strategies in Mexican new society. I will call these "desperate bets," wherein the outside options are either to leave or to raise a voice of protest. The middle strategy is hedging, where, in the face of adversity, neither exit nor voice nor a strong version of loyalty is exercised, but rather a strategy of survival is quietly sought through the diversification of "strategic bets."

The consideration that motivates the amendment I have added to Hirschman's model relates to actors' social networks, regardless of the decaying institution they are dealing with as individual workers or employees. My idea is that, due in part to the fact that Mexico has never had a regime that strives for and approximates the instatement of the rule of law, and in part to the preponderance of informal economies, social actors in Mexico tend to react to institutional decay not as individuals but as members of families or groups of friends and relations. This inflects individual economic strategies and leads to the prevalence of the fourth option that must be added to Hirschman's 'exit, voice, and loyalty,' and which might be characterized as a variant of what James Scott famously called the "weapons of the weak," that is, strategies that are geared toward reducing labor commitments to an employer or an institution without leaving the job or openly rebelling against current conditions.[4] Scott considered these practices as forms of resistance. I understand them rather as modalities of resentment and alienation that are oriented toward freeing up time for other activities, which may or may not be economically profitable but will serve to deepen or widen the actor's social network. I believe that calling this kind of strategy "resistance," as Scott did, frames it in a very specific teleology, which is that of the class struggle, when the same action can also be narrated in another way, as an episode of the heroic saga of upholding the family order, for instance, or honoring a friendship network.

Thus, although the popular Mexican proverb "You pretend to pay me, and I'll pretend to work" speaks a stance of resistance against the employer on the part of the worker, the tactic may also be understood as an attitude that is oriented toward upholding labor diversification. This is a common family strategy, used to overcome collective adversity and allow the family to continue in a viable—and ideally a pleasant—space for enjoyment and reproduction. In such situations, workers neither raise their voices against their employer nor quit their jobs but, instead, seek to reduce their investments in the job, in order to cultivate supplementary activities. This is a strategy in which a little loyalty to the employer may exist, perhaps, but not deep loyalty. In other words, the parameter of loyalty to the employer or the employing institution does not wholly disappear, so long as the person chooses to keep the job. Notably, this kind of practical orientation is not exclusively provoked by miserable salaries—though poor salaries are pervasive in Mexico. Hedging can become a general social orientation when the informal network of family, friends, and allies is the key referent in making work decisions.

Grand récit and Contingency

We are living in a time characterized by institutional instability that has been provoked by deep economic changes and a transformation of the very architecture of the state, including the abandonment of some of the state's traditional functions, such as that of being the guarantor of public security. It is no coincidence that this is also an era of great teleological narratives: instability must be interpreted and thereby normalized. During the first portion of Mexico's contemporary transformation, the neoliberal transition, with all its disorder, was told as the story of the democratic transition, while the current, second moment of change is prone to calling itself the culmination or "fourth phase" in a two-hundred-year history of national emancipation. It is striking how important teleology is in an era that is characterized by so much uncertainty.

Because teleology proposes a plot, a direction, for history, it is logical that it played an important role in the two stages of political and economic reform that have unfolded since Mexico's 1982 fiscal crisis and the subsequent advent of neoliberal and post-neoliberal reforms. Major changes always go hand in hand with what the French call a *grand récit*, or a master narrative. Such stories provide social actors with a sense of purpose and direction: democratic transition and modernization, for some, and the completion of national emancipation—with its obsession with "the recovery of sovereignty"—for others.

Regardless of how viable, realistic, or desirable the direction set by these two narratives has been, these teleologies also have another function, which is to get people to turn a blind eye— or at least to tolerate—the inability of the Mexican state to mitigate the catastrophic results of the various policies it has put in place. The changes that have taken place in Mexico over the past forty years have displaced masses of people, provoked bankruptcies, and led to the unrestricted use of violence as an instrument with which to order economic spaces. Teleology— in our case, the beautiful story either of the democratic transition or of the recovery of sovereignty under the aegis of the so-called Fourth Transformation—serves to minimize these facts, which appear slight in comparison with the lofty goals that are on the horizon. The inability of Mexican governments to deal with the minor—and sometimes not so very minor— daily catastrophes that reverberate throughout the country is the echo chamber in which this hollow rhetoric resonates.

Here is a recent example. On September 30, 2021, news broke out that in Iguala (Guerrero state), a criminal organization calling itself Los Tlacos captured, tortured, and executed twenty-one alleged hit men from another organization, called La Bandera, on camera, and uploaded the video to YouTube.[5] Three days later, on October 2, in order to commemorate the anniversary of the 1968 Tlatelolco student massacre, the president of Mexico signed with great fanfare a decree to create the Commission for Access to the Truth and the Historical Clarification and Promotion of Justice for Serious Human Rights Violations Committed between 1965 and 1990.[6] The juxtaposition of these two events, which coincided in time almost to the day, is a perfect example of the relationship between solemn ritual performances of teleology and lack of governmental control. Mexico's government is unable to mount an effective or even vaguely credible criminal investigation into a live-streamed massacre of twenty-one people, so it shifts attention to ritually redeeming the state's past crimes, which it blames for all current ills, and continues on that basis to promise a bright future. In Mexico today, killings follow one after the other without restraint or consequence. This week's massacre erases the memory of last week's. Impunity for murder continues to hover around 96 percent, as has been the case for years, and the capacity to guarantee peace in regions like Iguala remains nil. But none of this prevents the solemn commemoration of the anniversary of the massacre of October 2, 1968—which left fewer dead than there are murders in Mexico today in any given week—complete with new decrees to get to the "real truth" of what happened between 1965 and 1990, when the episodes of coercion occurred that are used to justify the changes introduced by the current government and its views concerning the direction of History, with a capital *H*. "Things are out of control," they sometimes acknowledge, "but we are paying for the crimes of the past"; "There is lack of control, but we are doing well."

Teleology in Mexico today is suffused with either bad faith or wishful thinking. Government enthusiasts like to fill the air with lengthy sermons on History, in order to minimize the disastrous effects of government policies. They then present them either as the lesser evil or as a delayed effect of the previous system for which the current government bears no blame. It is never accepted that today's dead, today's displaced, today's disappeared, today's bankruptcies, today's migrations might be at least in part the responsibility of today's government, let alone of today's state. We have governments that have been implementing important changes in the very structure of the state, without the instruments required to prevent or mitigate some of those changes' catastrophic results. Teleology serves to distract us from this basic fact.

Here are more examples. Migration agreements are reached with the United States that transfer the regulation of migratory flows from the southern US border to Mexico's southern border, and Chiapas instantly becomes the prey of organized crime to such an extent that the Zapatistas now warn that the region is on the brink of civil war.[7] What has the "democratic transition" or the "Fourth Transformation" to do with either the cause or the solution to this situation? Nothing. Similarly, there are press reports that the current government's Trans-Isthmic Railroad megaproject has attracted the Sinaloa Cartel, the Cartel Jalisco Nueva Generación, and other smaller criminal organizations to the Isthmus of Tehuantepec (Oaxaca and Veracruz states), where they are vying for control not only of the territory but of all the business that stems from the government project.[8] Again, just how do Mexico's two competing master narratives help us understand and alleviate these disturbing developments? The answer, again, is that they do not.

Finally, a third example: in August 2020, the Mexican Commission for the Defense and Promotion of Human Rights (CMDPDH) announced that the number of internally displaced people in Mexico reached 346,000, many of whom are from regions such as Guerrero and Chiapas, where the government, instead of being an effective regulator of the informal and illicit economies, is just one more violent actor.[9] Along with homicides and violent disappearances, forced displacement is a dramatic symptom of the catastrophic consequences of having a state that lacks the wherewithal to govern on the basis of its own normative framework. And such catastrophic examples of regulatory failure are always accompanied by a series of smaller catastrophes, less horrifying in scale, perhaps, but of great consequence: bankruptcies, unemployment, mounting suicide rates in Indigenous communities, health crises that ruin entire families.

The state's sustained investment in teleology—in the Master Narrative—seeks magically to reduce each and every one of these large and small catastrophes into events that are of secondary importance, regrettable but passing trifles. Rather than being faced as structural, foreseeable effects toward which the Mexican state has some responsibility, they are just regrettable aftershocks of the sins of prior governments, or of local deviations from morality, of the opposition's bad faith, or even of terrorism and sabotage. Organized crime must "learn to behave," as it did, according to the president of the republic, during the mid-term elections held in 2021, where the governing party held sway.[10] The ninety politicians who were murdered in the run-up to those very elections did not compel the president to acknowledge that the conditions under which those elections transpired are incompatible with democratic competition and, indeed, organized crime was even praised by the president because, from his point of view, things could have been worse (his party might, perhaps, have lost).[11] The mass migrations coming into Mexico from Central and South America and the Caribbean, too, are portrayed as barely "a crisis"—although they are already a regular and even predictable phenomenon, tied to demography, climate change, and state weakness in those countries.[12] The same rhetorical stance is taken with regard to pollution, the water crisis, and climate change. All of those potentially catastrophic developments pale in significance when put next to the stories of the democratic transition or the Fourth Transformation.

The reception and political processing of the COVID-19 pandemic played out in this very same context, which is why it was represented as "a contingency." In Mexico, contingency is a figure of public discourse that harks back to the so-called environmental contingencies—poor-air-quality days—that were routinely monitored and declared in Mexico City since the 1980s. Both examples of "contingency" (COVID and monitoring air quality) reflect Mexico's participation in a globalized world economy from which the country cannot escape. And both have in common, too, that they were faced as if the only relevant action that the national community can take is to swallow the bitter pill, put up with the alleged "contingency," and keep to the path that has been laid out in the master narrative, that the government repeats ever more insistently and with ever more cynicism: contingencies come and go, but our national destiny remains unperturbed.

The Historicity of the Pandemic and the Consolidation of "Contingency" as an Ethos

The concept of historicity refers to the ways in which the past and the future are mobilized in the present. Historicity is therefore a concept that recognizes that, among humans, the present is always infused both with the past—which manifests as "experience"—and the future—which makes itself present in the form of any number of expectations. Historicity, then, is the double horizon of the experiences and expectations that are mobilized in the present. In order to manage the COVID-19 pandemic, the government drew on a horizon of experience and on the management of expectations that had been forged in previous years, which can be summed up in one key word: *contingency*.

Indeed, contingency is a notion that has some very useful features for the new state. First, it refers to a random, and yet unavoidable, event that can make itself present at any time— you know that contingencies will happen, you just don't know when. Second, contingency suggests that the regrettable ("contingent") event will be of limited duration: contingencies pass and normality returns. Third, the people who are directly harmed by contingencies are not victims of the state; rather, in some cases, those victims can be imagined as being responsible for their own fate, as, for example, when Mexico's president suggested at the beginning of the pandemic that a very good protection for the citizenry against COVID was to remain faithful to the tenets of his electoral promises: never lie, never steal, never betray.[13] The implication was that popular imitation of the president's upright character and loyalty to his political program were somehow guarantees against contagion.

Contingency thus promotes a pragmatic orientation to risk that can be useful for coping with the anxiety and distress wrought by unpredictable dangers. It also serves to uphold a governance strategy that stresses the randomness of contingency rather than its predictable aspects, while circumventing any governmental responsibility in the matter. This involves normalizing and standardizing contingency and carrying out visible governmental actions to show that the government does indeed provide some sort of protection, even if it is usually ex post facto. In Mexico the political practice of contingency was normalized in the course of several decades that were dotted by days with dangerously high levels of air pollution, which were treated as if they were in themselves unavoidable, while the government humanely applied some provisional ameliorating measures, such as sounding off "red light" warnings.

This lengthy education naturalized the idea and governmental management of contingency. Just as today can be either cloudy or sunny, so too might it be dangerously smoggy. That's how it is with the weather. Just as today the dangers of COVID are inordinately high, so too will they dissipate tomorrow. Just as today everything is peaceful, tomorrow there may be a road-block or a shooting. Everything is normal, everything is natural, everything that is catastrophic is unavoidable. Thus, public health policies provided a kind of sentimental education in the management of catastrophe.

The government's material investment in the supposed inevitability of the COVID tragedy, where Mexico suffered some of the greatest losses worldwide, were not minor. In the early days of the pandemic, López Obrador recommended protecting oneself with amulets—the *detente* charm for warding off the devil, in particular—a gesture that was tantamount to recognizing that the disease was a matter of Divine Wrath.[14] The same sort of rationale is frequently applied in cases of disappearance, kidnapping, or murder where the victim is suspected of having had a hand in his or her fate: "En algo andaría" (S/he must have been involved in something). The government was invested in portraying the catastrophes that flowed from the pandemic as bad luck because ultimately what was at stake was its disinvestment from one of the core responsibilities of the welfare state—social medicine and the protection of life. As a symptom of this retraction, the president was presented by the Ministry of Health as a force of positive "moral contagion," who would not wear a face mask because his free-flowing breath would infect the population not with COVID, but rather with his fighting spirit.

The success of the idea of contingency, that is, of the absolution of the state from a number of responsibilities, was predicated on the fact that the country was already accustomed to an underperforming state, as well as on the fact that the population was used to making family decisions based on considerations that are very similar to the idea of contingency. This is why this notion so well summarizes the spirit of the times—it points to both a governance strategy and a pragmatic orientation of individuals, families, and social groups.

Hedging

The diversification of bets—a series of strategies that has been formalized in the world of finance around a concept that comes from gambling—*hedging* refers to the practice of reducing the risk of catastrophic loss through a portfolio with counterbalanced investments. I invest a lot of money in clean energy, but I also invest a somewhat smaller amount, say, in an automobile company that makes cars with both electric and gasoline engines, so that if my wager on clean energy does not succeed, it is hedged by my side bet on the gasoline engine. One risk is offset by the other.

This kind of diversification of economic stakes has always been a decisive strategy for Mexican families. In the mid-twentieth century, for example, it was common for peasant families—parents and older siblings—to invest in the education of one of the younger children, so that he or she could study to be a schoolteacher, which was a short and comparatively inexpensive career that provided modest but secure income. In this way, the family sought to assure some fixed income—a government salary—to reduce the insecurity that is intrinsic to the peasant economy. It is no coincidence that states with a robust peasantry, such as Oaxaca, Guerrero, Chiapas, and Michoacán, also have disproportionately large numbers of teachers, nor that the Oaxacan peasantry has tended to support the local teachers' union in its frequent and protracted strikes, even when this strategy affects their children's education.

It was also common for peasant families to send a daughter to work as a domestic servant in the city, due to restrictions on women's access to the labor market. Through such strategies of selective rural-to-urban migration, peasant families reduced their daily expenses—the migration of the young woman would mean one less mouth to feed—while it gained her family occasional monetary supports. The stark oppression that female domestic workers have faced throughout Mexican history has compounded almost total vulnerability to employee exploitation with the guilt-fueled extortion to which those women have often been subjected by their parents and siblings.

Migration to the United States, which until a few decades ago tended in many migrants' imaginations or desires to be "circular," with many comings and goings between the United States and Mexico, also fit into this logic of investment diversification, or hedging: if there was unemployment in the United States, there was familial support available back in Mexico, where the migrant did not pay rent, enjoyed the warmth of belonging, and had low living costs. The migrant worker, in turn, contributed resources to pay the extraordinary costs of family and community reproduction—weddings, baptisms, quinceañeras, and patron saint celebrations, for instance—and provided moneys for the modernization and improvement of his house: the purchase of electrical appliances, the construction of a second story, and so on. It is no coincidence that one of Mexico's greatest fortunes—that of Ricardo Salinas Pliego—was built on a company, Elektra, and its money-wiring bank, designed to funnel migrant remittances into the purchase of furniture and home appliances through a system of credit and monthly payments. Nor is it a coincidence that this same man's bank, Banco Azteca, which was founded to facilitate and exploit the flow of remittances from the United States to Mexico, has been chosen by the current government to manage government transfers through the so-called Banco del Bienestar. There is an overlap between the network of coverage provided by migrants and the political clientele that both neoliberal and post-neoliberal governments have been building through direct transfer programs.

In the informal economy, employment diversification has been crucial for families, as Larissa Adler Lomnitz showed in her 1975 book on "how the marginalized survive."[15] People in the informal economy are reliant on the support of their neighbors and relatives because their jobs are uncertain. Indeed, the informal economy is built on social networks characterized by *internal diversification*, that is, by something like the "hedging" that financial experts are so interested in today: when one worker has little work, he or she can be supported by another.

It is this diversification of strategies at the family level that leads me to propose a friendly amendment to Hirschman's model: a worker who survives thanks to her network can face worsening working conditions without resorting to either voice or exit, or to a positive affirmation of loyalty. Individuals may put up with declining conditions if their position within a broader network makes the job convenient for a diversified network. In the face of adversity, a member of a family that is used to operating as part of such an economic unit can endure more than a worker ascribed to one of the family models that have become the normative prototype in the formal economy—for instance, nuclear families that depend on the income of the father or mother or both, or single person households.

Even so, Mexico's middle and upper classes too have relied on strategies analogous to those we observe in the informal economy: investments in conspicuous consumption—cars and clothes, for instance—or in parties and restaurants, geared toward strengthening the chances of a profitable marriage for a son or daughter. In the middle classes, supplementing income through activities complementary to the main job is common—whether through selling home-baked goods or through participation in multilevel marketing companies such as Amway or Herbalife, which use the social networks of their "associates" to market their products. There is a telling fusion in such companies between formal business and an informal social organization, expressed in their peculiar corporate languages, wherein every employee or salesperson is considered a "partner" or "associate," rather than an employee, and every customer is a potential partner. It is no coincidence that another of Mexico's major home-grown corporations, Omnilife, is precisely this kind of business, nor should we be surprised by the success of the so-called gig economy that organizes, standardizes, commercializes, and extracts rent from what had been routine forms of labor diversification in both the informal economy and the middle classes.

The Mexican middle classes have wide-ranging investments in social networks, which is diversification as a survival strategy.

This is due not only to the importance of networks for successful placement in the labor market but also to the importance of personal relationships in dealing with a state that has never upheld the rule of law, understood here as a principle wherein people and institutions are all equally subject to the law. For the middle classes, having (informal) access to government agencies through acquaintances may be crucial to acquiring a permit to open a business, speeding up a legal procedure, gaining access to a public hospital, or to information that is indispensable for winning a government contract, for example.

For their part, the formal working classes too have depended on family diversification, and this is true even of the industrial working class. In Mexico, trade unions have been, to a significant extent, family businesses and, beyond that, skilled industrial workers have had—from a family angle at least—an assured passage to the middle classes, so that working families operate with strategies identical to those we have already identified in both the peasantry and the middle classes.

In short, Mexican society as a whole has developed forms of sociability oriented toward reciprocity, sustaining social networks, and cultivating internal diversification in those networks. This explains the passion that existed in Mexico around presidential successions in the era when there was no democracy, when Mexico had a one-party system (roughly 1929–94). Everyone knew or supposed that the official party would remain in power, and that the outgoing president would handpick his successor, but the identity of the successor was unknown until it was officially announced. The decision affected a broad social sector because each candidate had his or her own network that was internally diversified, and each member of that network, in turn, had his or her own network. This is why the so-called *destape* (the unveiling of the presidential successor) was a much more widely speculative, more interesting, event than is often remembered. It was an occasion for each person or family to think about whether they had some direct or indirect contact somewhere in the government: if not with the president, then perhaps with an undersecretary; if not with the secretary, then maybe with an office director; or with the trusted ally of the trusted ally of some government employee. The political system was authoritarian, certainly, but it mobilized the social networks of a thick layer of middle and even popular sectors. And that is how Mexico was once governed. It was a system built on a social organization that was not very individualistic but instead characterized by internally differentiated social networks in which each actor sought some "hedge" to fend off any potentially catastrophic contingency, such as unemployment. Mexican society's propensity for diversification as a family strategy has been the reason for its resilience, but it has also naturalized a rhetoric of contingency that is now being deployed in the face of the state's retraction from its responsibility to guarantee a minimum of security and justice.

So What Happened?

My starting point in these lectures has been that the liberalization of the economy in the 1980s and 1990s led to bankruptcies of such a magnitude that they placed entire sectors of the population in the situation envisaged in Albert Hirschman's model:

voice or exit seemed inevitable, and simple loyalty seemed no longer possible. Up until that time, in Mexico such stark choices (exit or voice) had been inhibited by the prevalence of family-based or friendship-based hedging strategies, most particularly in sectors of precarious employment, such as the activities of the informal economy and those of the peasantry, but also in the formal working class and the middle classes.

The number of bankruptcies in the countryside—both among peasants and in ranch economies—in many cases meant that traditional strategies to diversify the family net-

work were no longer sufficient, and many people now faced the Hirschmanian alternative of exit or voice. Moreover, exit in the form of an emigration would no longer be circular, but might even imply the outright abandonment of the family to seek out individual alternatives. Young people could no longer aspire to the adult status of head of household, for instance. Migrant women or "unaccompanied minors" seeking their fortunes or, in the case of the violently displaced communities of the past few years, the emigration of entire families would have no pos-sibility of return.

The situation of "exit" from the family institution is one of the major research topics that is required in order to under-stand what has sometimes been referred to as Mexico's torn so-cial fabric because, given the limits of the family diversification strategy, the traditional family form has shown itself to be pre-carious. Family breakdown can be triggered by the decisions of isolated family members—instances in which decisions to mi-grate are no longer made in the framework of family reproduc-tion strategies. Family breakdown can also operate from the outside in, so to speak, when cartels recruit young people, or even kidnap them, into a violent organization that is figured as if it were a new family but that almost never allows the young recruit to achieve the fulfilment associated with full adulthood: reproduction. In other words, the precariousness of the family as a reproductive unit is manifest in ways wherein "exit" frequently is not the product of the individual's decision, but is rather the failure of entire families and communities to defend themselves and retain their members.

In the case of the bankruptcies that occurred in the ranch economy of the 1980s and 1990s, the effects of the threat of family breakdown were somewhat different. Many ranches faced credit crises and bankruptcies precisely at a moment when drug trafficking profits were soaring. This coincidence led to a deep imbrication of the narcos into ranch economies. Drug producers and traffickers became moneylenders, acquired new properties or partnerships, and entered into businesses that had been the domain of the legal-economy *ranchero* class. They were then able to capitalize on the new agricultural export economies that became possible with NAFTA, in avocados or limes, for instance This situation increased the political influence of the illicit economies and made it more difficult to establish clear distinctions between what was legal and what was illegal, between mafia networks and political authority.

In some sectors of the economy, recourse to expressing a dissident "voice" was strongly inhibited by this integration between illicit and licit economies, and by the so-called capture of the state by criminal organizations. The suffusion of the economy with moneys from organized crime has indeed had complex implications for the public use of voice and, although protest increased dramatically alongside liberalization, so has its violent suppression, as can be documented by the staggering numbers of journalists, social activists, grass-roots environmental leaders, and local politicians who have been murdered. A sociology oriented to this question would be needed in order to understand specific characteristics of Mexico's democracy.

Indeed, the faith that was placed, during the first stage of the current transition, in the importation of capital as the only mechanism that was capable of guaranteeing a transition toward the rule of law also implied that the democratic transition was beyond the control of local forces. If NAFTA was the guarantor of democratic institution–building, this meant that government and societal forces could afford to play the tepid role of the "free rider." This unwillingness to take political risks in favor of strengthening the state's institutional armature has only become more pronounced in the current, allegedly postneoliberal, era, and this same aversion to risk also has limited the government's ability to deal with catastrophic situations. Today, in Mexico, there is a lot of protest and very little state response. The current situation, then, is characterized by new combinations of the alternatives discussed by Hirschman: there is much recourse to voice but little effectiveness of democratic participation; there is a strong impulse to abandon or to flee, but an increasingly constrained horizon of escape. There is deep know-how in the arts of hedging but limited ability to achieve the kind of diversification that guarantees stability.

This kind of context, which increasingly brings to mind a game of "musical chairs"—as dramatized globally in TV series such as *The Hunger Games* or *Squid Game*—has been administered in Mexico with a strategy of governance that legitimizes itself daily by appealing to contingency. Disaster here is the result of either bad luck or moral failure. The government complains of a moral crisis in society, of a torn social fabric, when what is really happening is that the state has relinquished several of its classic functions.

The ideology of contingency is a formula that reinforces the traditional mechanisms of familial survival—hence the constant praise and reinforcement of the traditional family, even by the current government—and at the same time, the emphasis on contingency allows the government to retain a modicum of rhetorical control in the face of our everyday disasters, even as the state tacitly, or even explicitly, declares itself incapable of seriously attacking the causes or mitigating the effects of disaster. The idea that Mexico's problems stem from a moral crisis—from a torn social fabric—is thus a key element of the ideology of a new state that has ceded key administrative responsibilities to the God of Contingency.

Notes

Lecture 1. Interpretation of the "Torn Social Fabric"

This lecture was delivered on March 5, 2021.

1 See, for a sociological argument, Sefchovic, *¡Atrévete! Propuesta hereje para disminuir la violencia en México*; in the public sphere, President López Obrador has made various pleas to Mexico's narcos to think of their mothers and of their families, and stop the violence.

2 Weiner and Schneider, *Cloth and Human Experience*.

3 Graeber and Sahlins, *On Kings*.

4 Graeber and Sahlins, *On Kings*, 3.

5 Raphael, "En México, todo el presupuesto al poder militar."

6 Rea and Ferri, *La tropa*, 537.

7 Rea and Ferri, *La tropa*, 537–38.

8 Rea and Ferri, *La tropa*, 447.

9 Pérez Correa, Silva Forné, and Gutiérrez Rivas, "Indice de letalidad."

10 Colón, "Relación del primer viaje de descubrimiento," 105 (my translation).

11 Lomnitz, "Acerca de la reciprocidad negativa."

12 Ward, *Gangsters without Borders*.

13 Friedrich, *Princes of Naranja*.

14 Nutini, *San Bernardino Contla*, 268.

15 See Arias, *Del arraigo a la diáspora*.

16 Blázquez, "The Continuum of Women's Abduction in Mexico."

Lecture 2. The State Estranged from Itself

This lecture was delivered on June 25, 2021.

1 Ortega y Gasset, *Invertebrate Spain.*

2 Abrams, "Notes on the Difficulty of Studying the State."

3 Espíndola Mata, *El hombre que podía todo, todo, todo,* 15.

4 Freud, "The Uncanny"; Lacan, *Anxiety,* 41–49, 74–76.

5 Sabet, *Police Reform in Mexico.*

6 Sabet, *Police Reform in Mexico,* 8.

7 González González, *Lo negro del Negro Durazo,* 17.

8 Magaloni, "Arbitrariness and Inefficiency in the Mexican Criminal Justice System," 91.

9 A similar process occurred in Guadalajara as well. See Suárez de Garay, *Los policías,* 9.

10 Arteaga Botello and López Rivera, "El aprendizaje de un policía."

11 Arteaga Botellos and López Rivera, "Viaje al interior de la policía."

12 Suárez de Garay, *Los policías,* 152–53.

13 Suárez de Garay, *Los policías,* 151.

14 López-Portillo, "Accounting for the Unaccountable," 107.

15 Suárez de Garay, *Los policías,* 176.

16 Arteaga Botello and López Rivera, "El aprendizaje de un policía" [Don't argue with your direct superiors, the person on guard, officers, or any senior colleague because the ranking official is always right (my translation)].

17 Arteaga Botello and López Rivera, "El aprendizaje de un policía."

18 Suárez de Garay, *Los policías,* 195.

19 Arteaga Botello and López Rivera, "El aprendizaje de un policía."

20 Suárez de Garay, *Los policías,* 187.

21 Arteaga Botello and López Rivera, "El aprendizaje de un policía."

22 Arteaga Botello and López Rivera, "El aprendizaje de un policía."

23 López-Portillo, "Accounting for the Unaccountable," 110.

24 Arteaga Botello and López Rivera, "El aprendizaje de un policía."

25 Arteaga Botello and López Rivera, "El aprendizaje de un policía."

Lecture 3. The Armed Wing of the Informal Economy

This lecture was delivered on July 30, 2021.

1 Azaola Garrido, *Imagen y autoimagen de la policía de la Ciudad de México*, 37–38.

2 Treviño Rangel and Velázquez Moreno, "Torture and the Military in Mexico's War on Drugs," 12.

3 Azaola Garrido, *Imagen y autoimagen de la policía de la Ciudad de México*, 59.

4 Giacomello, *Un pie en la cárcel y otro en el panteón.*

5 Contreras-Velasco, "Institución policial," 699.

6 Gilet, "La seguridad privada creció más que las fuerzas policiales."

7 Maldonado, "'You Don't See Any Violence Here,'" 159.

8 Padilla Reyes and Arteaga Botello, "Códigos de la violencia," 24–45.

9 Grandmaison, "Drug Cartels, from Political to Criminal Intermediation," 28–29; Geffray, "State, Wealth and Criminals."

10 Maldonado, "'You Don't See Any Violence Here,'" 160, 166.

11 Padilla Reyes and Arteaga Botello, "Códigos de violencia," 35, 41.

12 Zepeda Lecuona, *Crimen sin castigo.*

13 López-Portillo, "Accounting for the Unaccountable," 109.

14 Pérez Correa, "Criminal Investigation and Prosecution in Mexico City," 78.

15 Smith, *The Dope.*

16 Smith, *The Dope*, 321.

17 Friedrich, *Agrarian Revolt in a Mexican Village*; see also Friedrich, *The Princes of Naranja.*

18 On the DFS badges carried by three of the armed men guarding El Búfalo, see Smith, *The Dope*, 330; on the conditions at the ranch during Caro Quintero's time, see Mayorga, "Búfalo hoy."

19 Smith, *The Dope*, 338.

20 Aguayo Quezada, *La charola*, 245.

21 Smith, *The Dope*, 257.

22 Zavala, *Los cárteles no existen.*

23 Correa-Cabrera, *Los Zetas Inc.*

Lecture 4. Regional Systems of the Criminal Economy

This lecture was delivered on August 27, 2021.

1   Skinner, "Marketing and Social Structure in Rural China."

2   Fernando Escalante Gonzalbo was the first, and most cogent, scholar to raise an alert regarding security experts' propagandistic representations of crime (see *El crimen como realidad y como representación*); the use of this sort of justified and pertinent criticism was taken a step further, though, to the point of raising doubts concerning the very existence of complex social organizations orchestrating illicit economies (see Zavala, *Los cárteles no existen*).

3   DEA, "2020 National Drug Threat Assessment," 4.

4   For an overview, see Azaola Garrido, "Panorama general del sistema penitenciario en México," 41. Regarding torture, Azaola Garrido mentions that INEGI's 2016 national survey found that "59 percent [of inmates] reported that they had been kicked and beaten, 39 percent were beaten with objects [such as police batons, bats, etc.], and 19 percent reported that they had received electric shock treatments, among other torture methods" (40–41).

5   Asmann, "Metamphetamine Is New Drug of Choice in Mexico's Domestic Market."

6   Ward, *Gangsters without Borders*, 170.

7   Rafael, *The Mexican Mafia*, 160.

8   Rafael, *The Mexican Mafia*, 140–41.

9   Interview with Fernando Montero, August 13, 2021. Montero was part of a research team that explored the relationship between urban segregation and the heroin market; the team showed that—throughout the East Coast—heroin distribution flows from dilapidated Puerto Rican neighborhoods outward, to other ethnic neighborhoods. See Rosenblum et al., "Urban Segregation and the Heroin Market."

10   Lomnitz, "Los orígenes de nuestra supuesta homogeneidad."

11   Rafael, *The Mexican Mafia*, 44.

12   Rafael, *The Mexican Mafia*, 226.

13   Rafael, *The Mexican Mafia*, 225; see also Mozingo, "Highland Park Gang Trial Paints a Landscape of Hate."

14 Rafael, *The Mexican Mafia*, 155.

15 Moreno, *Me dicen: "El más loco."*

16 For brief descriptions of the activities of Mexican cartels in the region, see Dudley, "The Zetas in Guatemala (Parts I, II, and III)"; Silva Ávalos, "Arrests Could Strengthen Links between Tony Hernández and Sinaloa Cartel in Honduras."

17 Ayuso, "Why Did the Game Change in Honduras?"

18 Zuidema, "Hierarchy and Space in Incaic Social Organization."

19 Ayuso, "Why Did the Game Change in Honduras?," 4.

20 See Silva Ávalos, "Arrests Could Strengthen Links between Tony Hernández and Sinaloa Cartel in Honduras."

21 Dudley, in "The Zetas in Guatemala," writes, "Contrary to many reports surfacing that the Zetas seek street gang members for hire, two former government officials told *InSight Crime* that the Zetas prefer ex-soldiers precisely because they come with some training, skills, and weapons, and an understanding of hierarchical management."

Lecture 5. Island of Rights, Sea of Extortion

This lecture was delivered on September 24, 2021.

1 LaClau, *On Populist Reason.*

2 Graeber and Sahlins, *On Kings*, 5.

3 Halbertal, *On Sacrifice*, 10–13.

Lecture 6. Contingency as the New Zeitgeist

This lecture was delivered on October 29, 2021.

1 Lomnitz, "Tierra caliente" and "Michoacán."

2 Hirschman, *Exit, Voice, and Loyalty.*

3 I owe the idea of seeing *hedging* in the financial arena as a form of evasion to Dr. Alejandra Azuero, who presented this idea at the "Evasion Workshop," organized by Kevin O'Neill, on September 24, 2021.

4 Scott, *Weapons of the Weak.*

5 Castañeda and García, "La violencia se recrudece en Iguala con la matanza de sicarios de cárteles rivales."

6 "Investigarán violaciones a derechos humanos durante la 'Guerra Sucia."

7 Hernández Navarro, "Chiapas, de paramilitares a crimen organizado"; Zurita Sahagún, "Chiapas es un polvorín."

8 Riva Palacio, "El mensaje del presidente."

9 Anaya, "México acumula 346 mil desplazados internos."

10 "Delincuencia organizada se 'portó bien' en elecciones."

11 Arista, "Con 90 políticos asesinados, en 2021."

12 Escalante Gonzalbo, "No es una crisis."

13 "'No mentir, no robar y no traicionar ayuda mucho para que no dé coronavirus.'"

14 Badillo, "AMLO y sus polémicas declaraciones sobre el coronavirus."

15 Published in English as *Networks and Marginality*.

Bibliography

Abrams, Phillip. "Notes on the Difficulty of Studying the State." *Journal of Historical Sociology* 1, no. 1 (1988): 58–89.

Aguayo Quezada, Sergio. *La charola: Una historia de los servicios de inteligencia en México*. Mexico City: Editorial Grijalbo, 2001.

Anaya, Samantha. "México acumula 346 mil desplazados internos: CMDPDH." *ZonaDocs*, August 20, 2020. https://www.zonadocs.mx/2020/08/20/mexico-acumula-346-mil-desplazados-internos-cmdpdh/.

Arias, Patricia. *Del arraigo a la diáspora: Dilemas de la familia rural*. Mexico City: Miguel Angel Porrúa, 2009.

Arista, Lidia. "Con 90 políticos asesinados, en 2021, las campañas más violentas desde 2000." *Expansión Política*, June 5, 2021. https://politica.expansion.mx/mexico/2021/06/05/voces-90-politicos-asesinados-en-2021-las-campanas-mas-violentas-desde-2000.

Arteaga Botello, Nelson, and Adrián López Rivera. "El aprendizaje de un policía." *Nexos*, August 1, 1998.

Arteaga Botello, Nelson, and Adrián López Rivera. "Viaje al interior de la policía: El caso de un municipio de México." *Nexos*, April 1, 1998.

Asmann, Parker. "Methamphetamine Is New Drug of Choice in Mexico's Domestic Market." *Mexico News Daily*, May 8, 2021. https://mexiconewsdaily.com/news/methamphetamine-is-new-drug-of-choice/.

Ayuso, Tomás. "Why Did the Game Change in Honduras?" Unpublished ms., 2017.

Azaola Garrido, Elena. *Imagen y autoimagen de la policía de la Ciudad de México*. Mexico City: CIESAS, 2005.

Azaola Garrido, Elena. "Panorama general del sistema penitenciario en México." In *Entrecruces entre delito, justicia y sistema carcelario: Perspectivas multidisciplinares*, edited by Martha Chávez Torres, Isabel Juárez Becerra, and Rocío Camacho Rojas, 37–50. Zamora: El Colegio de Michoacán, 2023.

Badillo, Diego. "AMLO y sus polémicas declaraciones sobre el coronavirus." *El Economista*, March 21, 2020. https://www.eleconomista.com.mx/politica/AMLO-y-sus-polemicas-declaraciones-sobre-el-coronavirus-20200321-0001.html.

Blázquez, Adele. "The Continuum of Women's Abduction in Mexico: Porosities between Sexual and Armed Violence in a Drug-Producing Area (Badiraguato, Sinaloa)." *Dialectical Anthropology* 45 (2021): 233–51.

Castañeda, María Julia, and Jacobo García. "La violencia se recrudece en Iguala con la matanza de sicarios de cárteles rivales." *El País*, September 30, 2021.

Colón, Cristóbal. "Relación del primer viaje de descubrimiento." In *Relaciones y cartas*, 105. Madrid: Librería de la viuda de Hernando y Cª, 1892.

Contreras-Velasco, Óscar. "Institución policial, violencia y cultura del terror en Tijuana." *Revista Mexicana de Sociología* 79, no. 4 (2017): 697–721.

Correa-Cabrera, Guadalupe. *Los Zetas Inc.: Criminal Corporations, Energy, and Civil War in Mexico*. Austin: University of Texas Press, 2017.

DEA (Drug Enforcement Administration). "2020 National Drug Threat Assessment." Washington, DC: US Department of Justice—Drug Enforcement Administration, March 2021.

"Delincuencia organizada se 'portó bien' en elecciones, afirma López Obrador." *El Financiero*, June 7, 2021. https://www.elfinanciero.com.mx/elecciones-2021/2021/06/07/delincuencia-organizada-se-porto-bien-en-elecciones-afirma-lopez-obrador/.

Dudley, Steven. "The Zetas in Guatemala (Parts I, II, and III)." *InSight Crime*, September 8, 2011. https://insightcrime.org/investigations/the-zetas-in-guatemala/.

"El Salvador Profile." *InSight Crime*, September 15, 2020. https://insight crime.org/el-salvador-organized-crime-news/el-salvador/.

Escalante Gonzalbo, Fernando. *El crimen como realidad y como representación: Contribución para una historia del presente*. Mexico City: El Colegio de México, 2012.

Escalante Gonzalbo, Fernando. "No es una crisis." *Milenio*, September 15, 2021.

Espíndola Mata, Juan. *El hombre que podía todo, todo, todo: Ensayo sobre el mito presidencial en México*. Mexico City: El Colegio de México, 2004.

Freud, Sigmund. "The Uncanny." In *Freud Library 14: Art and Literature*, 339–76. 1919. London: Penguin, 1985.

Friedrich, Paul. *Agrarian Revolt in a Mexican Village*. Englewood Cliffs, NJ: Prentice Hall, 1970.

Friedrich, Paul. *The Princes of Naranja: An Essay in Ethnohistorical Method*. Austin: University of Texas Press, 1986.

Geffray, Christian. "State, Wealth, and Criminals." *Lusotopie* 9, no. 1 (2002): 83–106.

Giacomello, Corina. *Un pie en la cárcel y otro en el panteón: Testimonios de agentes del Ministerio Público, policías y peritos de la Procuraduría General de la República*. Mexico City: Tirant lo Blanch, 2018.

Gilet, Eliana. "La seguridad privada creció más que las fuerzas policiales de México durante la última década." *Sputnik International*, March 23, 2019. https://mundo.sputniknews.com/20190321/seguridad-privada -estado-mexico-muertes-torturas-1086226434.html.

González González, José. *Lo negro del Negro Durazo*. Mexico City: Editorial Posada, 1983.

Graeber, David, and Marshall Sahlins. *On Kings*. Chicago: University of Chicago Press, 2017.

Grandmaison, Romain Le Cour. "Drug Cartels, from Political to Criminal Intermediation: The Caballeros Templarios' Mirror Sovereignty in Michoacán, Mexico." Paper presented at the Violence and New Mores Seminar, Columbia University, 2021.

Halbertal, Moshe. *On Sacrifice*. Princeton, NJ: Princeton University Press, 2012.

Hernández Navarro, Luis. "Chiapas, de paramilitares a crimen organizado." *NODAL*, July 22, 2021. https://www.nodal.am/2021/07/chiapas -de-paramilitares-a-crimen-organizado-por-luis-hernandez-navarro/.

Hirschman, Albert O. *Exit, Voice, and Loyalty: Responses to Decline in Firms, Organizations, and States.* Cambridge, MA: Harvard University Press, 1970.

"Investigarán violaciones a derechos humanos durante la 'Guerra Sucia.'" *El Informador*, October 2, 2021. https://www.informador.mx /mexico/2-de-Octubre-Investigaran-violaciones-a-derechos-humanos -durante-Guerra-Sucia-20211002-0073.html.

Lacan, Jacques. *Anxiety: The Seminar of Jacques Lacan, Book 10.* Translated by A. R. Price. Cambridge: Polity, 2016.

LaClau, Ernesto. *On Populist Reason.* London: Verso, 2005.

Lomnitz, Claudio. "Acerca de la reciprocidad negativa." *Revista de Antropología Social* 14 (2005): 311–39.

Lomnitz, Claudio. "Los orígenes de nuestra supuesta homogeneidad: Breve arqueología de la unidad nacional en México." *Prismas* 14, no. 1 (2010): 17–36.

Lomnitz, Claudio. "Michoacán: Fantasía de la familia, fantasía del estado." In *La nación desdibujada: México en trece ensayos*, 13–40. Mexico City: Malpaso, 2016.

Lomnitz, Claudio. "Tierra caliente: Lectura en clave antropológica." *La Jornada,* January 22, 2014.

Lomnitz, Larissa Adler. *Networks and Marginality: Life in a Mexican Shantytown.* Translated by Cinna Lomnitz. New York: Academic, 1977.

López-Portillo, Ernesto. "Accounting for the Unaccountable: The Police in Mexico." In *Mexico's Security Failure: Collapse into Criminal Violence*, edited by Paul Kenny, Mónica Serrano, and Arturo C. Sotomayor, 107–21. New York: Routledge, 2011.

Magaloni, Ana Laura. "Arbitrariness and Inefficiency in the Mexican Criminal Justice System." In *Mexico's Security Failure: Collapse into Criminal Violence*, edited by Paul Kenny, Mónica Serrano, and Arturo C. Sotomayor, 89–106. New York: Routledge, 2011.

Maldonado, Salvador. "'You Don't See Any Violence Here but It Leads to

Very Ugly Things': Forced Solidarity and Silent Violence in Michoacán, Mexico." *Dialectical Anthropology* 38, no. 2 (2014): 153–71.

Mayorga, Patricia. "Búfalo hoy: El estigma del narco." *Proceso*, April 8, 2016. https://www.proceso.com.mx/reportajes/2016/4/8/bufalo-hoy -el-estigma-del-narco-162231.html.

Moreno, Nazario. *Me dicen: "El más loco."* Mexico City: Estudios Fotográficos Universal de Fran Tonebaum, 2011.

Mozingo, Joe. "Highland Park Gang Trial Paints a Landscape of Hate." *Los Angeles Times*, July 25, 2006.

"'No mentir, no robar y no traicionar ayuda mucho para que no dé coronavirus': AMLO." *Animal Político*, June 4, 2020. https://www .animalpolitico.com/2020/06/amlo-no-mentir-robar-traicionar-ayuda -contra-covid/.

Nutini, Hugo G. *San Bernardino Contla: Marriage and Family Structure in a Tlaxcalan Municipio*. Pittsburgh, PA: Pittsburgh University Press, 1968.

Ortega y Gasset, José. *Invertebrate Spain*. 1921. Translated by Mildred Adams. New York: W. W. Norton, 1937.

Padilla Reyes, Iliana del Rocío, and Nelson Arteaga Botello. "Códigos de violencia en espacios económicos en Culiacán, Sinaloa, México." *Revista de Sociología* 104, no. 1 (2019): 24–45.

Pérez Correa, Catalina. "Criminal Investigation and Prosecution in Mexico City: A Case Study of Miguel Hidalgo County and Its Ministerio Público." JD/PhD diss., Stanford University, 2006.

Pérez Correa, Catalina, Carlos Silva Forné, and Rodrigo Gutiérrez Rivas. "Indice de letalidad: Menos enfrentamientos, más opacidad." *Nexos*, July 1, 2015.

Rafael, Tony. *The Mexican Mafia*. New York: Encounter, 2007.

Raphael, Ricardo. "En México, todo el presupuesto al poder militar." *Washington Post* (Spanish edition), July 27, 2021. https://www.washing tonpost.com/es/post-opinion/2021/07/27/aumenta-presupuesto -militar-guardia-nacional-mexico-amlo/.

Rea, Daniela, and Pablo Ferri. *La tropa: Por qué mata un soldado*. Mexico City: Aguilar, 2018.

Riva Palacio, Raymundo. "El mensaje del presidente." *El Financiero*, De-

cember 16, 2021. https://www.elfinanciero.com.mx/opinion/raymun
do-riva-palacio/2021/12/16/el-mensaje-del-presidente/.

Rosenblum, Daniel, Fernando Montero Castrillo, Philippe Bourgois,
Sarah Mars, George Karandinos, George Jay Unick, and Daniel Cic-
carone. "Urban Segregation and the Heroin Market: A Quantitative
Model of Anthropological Hypotheses from an Inner-City Drugmar-
ket." *International Journal of Drug Policy* 25 (2014): 543–55.

Sabet, Daniel M. *Police Reform in Mexico: Informal Politics and the Challenge of Institutional Change*. Stanford, CA: Stanford University Press,
2012.

Scott, James C. *Weapons of the Weak: Everyday Forms of Peasant Resistance*. New Haven, CT: Yale University Press, 1985.

Sefchovic, Sarah. *¡Atrévete! Propuesta hereje para disminuir la violencia en
México*. Mexico City: Penguin Random House, 2014.

Silva Ávalos, Héctor. "Arrests Could Strengthen Links between Tony
Hernández and Sinaloa Cartel in Honduras." *InSight Crime*, June 18,
2020. https://insightcrime.org/news/brief/tony-hernandez-sinaloa-cartel
-honduras/.

Skinner, G. William. "Marketing and Social Structure in Rural China."
Journal of Asian Studies (1964–65). Reprinted in *Etudes Rurales* 161–62,
nos. 1–2 (2002): 215–61.

Smith, Benjamin T. *The Dope: The Real History of the Mexican Drug Trade*.
New York: W. W. Norton, 2021.

Suárez de Garay, María Eugenia. *Los policías: Una averiguación antropológica*. Guadalajara: ITESO, 2006.

Treviño-Rangel, Javier, Raúl Bejarano-Romero, Laura H. Atuesta, and Sara
Velázquez-Moreno. "Deadly Force and Denial: The Military's Legacy in
Mexico's 'War on Drugs.'" *International Journal of Human Rights*, 26, no.
4 (2022): 567–90. https://doi.org/10.1080/13642987.2021.1947806.

Treviño Rangel, Javier, and Sara Velázquez Moreno. "Torture and the Military in Mexico's War on Drugs." Unpublished ms., 2021.

Ward, T. W. *Gangsters without Borders: An Ethnography of a Salvadoran
Street Gang*. New York: Oxford University Press, 2013.

Weiner, Annette B., and Jane Schneider, eds. *Cloth and Human Experience.* Washington, DC: Smithsonian Institution, 1989.

Zavala, Oswaldo. *Los cárteles no existen: Narcotráfico y cultura en* México. Mexico City: Malpaso, 2018.

Zepeda Lecuona, Guillermo. *Crimen sin castigo: Procuración de justicia penal y ministerio público en México.* Mexico City: Fondo de Cultura Económica, 2004.

Zuidema, R. T. "Hierarchy and Space in Incaic Social Organization." *Ethnohistory* 30, no. 2 (1983): 49–75.

Zurita Sahagún, Ramón. "Chiapas es un polvorín." *Elpopular.mx,* October 22, 2021. https://elpopular.mx/opinion/2021/10/22/chiapas-es-un -polvorin.

Index

can state and, 2–3; municipal leaders' links to, 29–30; New Regime in Mexico and, 77–79; regional analysis of, 104–5, 111–34; resources for eradication of, 3; transnationalism of, 81, 94–100; US-Mexican relations and, 85–86, 95–96. *See also* cartels

drug lords (drug syndicates): appeals to mothers of, 4–5; caste superiority and, 11–12; police force and influence of, 76–77; as social bandits, 14–17; state connections with, 29–30; US alliances with, 99, 109–19

drug protection rackets, politics and, 85–93

drug trafficking: historical arc of, 104–9; in Honduras, 131–33; in Los Angeles, California, 109–19; regional subsystems for, 125–28; South and Central American networks for, 97–98; transition from state to federal control of, 85–93

Durazo, Arturo "El Negro," 36–39

Ebrard, Marcelo, 68

economic crises: bankruptcies and migration and, 191–95; hedging and, 186–91; police reforms and, 36–41

economic geography, negative reciprocity and, 14–17

economic space, neoliberalism and creation of, 139–40

egalitarianism, culture and, 7–8

El Búfalo marijuana ranch, 14–15, 91

El Colegio Nacional, ix, 28

elections: credibility of, 143; informal economy influence in, 74–77; organized crime and, 181–82

Elektra, 188

El infierno del Negro Durazo (comic book), 37–38

El Salvador, gangs from, 118–19, 133

El Sereno gang, 111

entrance examinations: payments for passing of, 56–57; police recruitment and, 45–47

Escalante Gonzalbo, Fernando, 200n2

Espíndola, Juan, 32–33

estrangement of the state, 31–35, 64, 162–64

ethnic enclaves: drug trafficking controlled by, 97; Los Angeles gangs and, 113–19. *See also* racial identity

exit: institutional decay and, 173–77; migration as, 192–95

export-based economy: Mexican infrastructure and, 148–51; state and, 147–48 extortion: informal economy and, 71–73; by LA gangs, 111–12; sea of vs. NAFTA islands, 153; by police, 52

extrajudicial killings, by Mexican military, 9–10

failed state, Mexico's image as, 8–9

familial mores: blood compensation and, 12; drug violence impact on, 1–2; exit from, 192–95; hedging and, 186–91; institutional decay and, 174–77; marriage practices and, 17–21; as organizational model, 171–72; war on drugs impact on, 3–6

Familia Michoacana (cartel), 127, 169, 172

favors: Judicial Police system of, 83; policy payment system for, 55–57

fayuca (US-made goods): border smuggling of and market for, 125–28

Federal Police, 9

fentanyl production, Mexican drug trafficking and, 135–36

Ferri, Pablo, 9–10

feud, as negative reciprocity, 12

fiscales (public prosecutors), 82

"Flowery War" (Aztec), 2–3

foreign investment: informal economies and, 151–53; NAFTA and, 149–51

Fourth Transformation, 145–46, 178–79, 180–81, ix

Fox, Vicente, 174

free trade zone: creation of, 139–40; Mexican state and, 155

Frenk, Julio, 143

Friedrich, Paul, 19, 21, 87

Fuerzas Especiales, 68

gangbanging, 117–18

gangs: artisanal local crime by, 81; in California, drug economy and, 110–19; cartels and, 16–17, 102–3; in Central America, 129–33; classification of, 102–3; illicit economies and, 15–17; regional organization of, 103. *See also individual gangs*

Garay, David, 67–68

García Abrego, Juan, 128

gas theft, 102

Geffrey, Christian, 78–79

geography of violence: negative reciprocity and, 14–17; in poppy-growing regions, 22–24; stealing women and, 17–21

Giacomello, Corina, 69–70

Girard, René, 12

global financial markets: illicit economies and, 144; Mexican state and, 139–40

Golden Triangle (drug-producing region), 120–21

González, Everardo, 40

221

223